JOOTHAN

Joothan

An Untouchable's Life

Omprakash Valmiki

Translated by Arun Prabha Mukherjee

COLUMBIA UNIVERSITY PRESS

New York

COLUMBIA UNIVERSITY PRESS
Publishers Since 1893
New York   Chichester, West Sussex

Joothan: An Untouchable's Life was first published
by Samya, an imprint of Bhatkal and Sen,
16 Southern Avenue, Kolkata 700 026, India, in 2003.
This edition is not for sale in South Asia.
This translation is from the original Hindi text, *Joothan*, by Omprakash
Valmiki, published by Radhakrishna Prakashan Pvt. Ltd., Delhi 1997.

Library of Congress Cataloging-in-Publication Data

Valmiki, Omprakasa 1950–
   [Joothan. English]
   Joothan/Omprakash Valmiki; translated by Arun Prabha Mukherjee.
      p. cm.
   Includes bibliographical references.
   ISBN 978-0-231-12972-5 (cloth : alk. paper)
   ISBN 978-0-231-12973-2 (pbk. : alk. paper)
   ISBN 978-0-231-50337-2 (e-book)
   1. Dalits—India—History. I. Mukherjee, Arun Prabha. II. Title.
DS422.C3V275 2003
305.5′122′0954—dc21   2002041710

DESIGNED BY LISA CHOVNICK

Columbia University Press books are printed on
permanent and durable acid-free paper.
Printed in the United States of America
c 10 9 8 7 6 5 4 3 2 1
p 10 9 8 7 6 5 4 3 2 1

For Ma and Pitaji

CONTENTS

FOREWORD
by Arun Prabha Mukherjee
IX

PREFACE TO THE HINDI EDITION
XIII

INTRODUCTION
by Arun Prabha Mukherjee
XVII

JOOTHAN
I

GLOSSARY
155

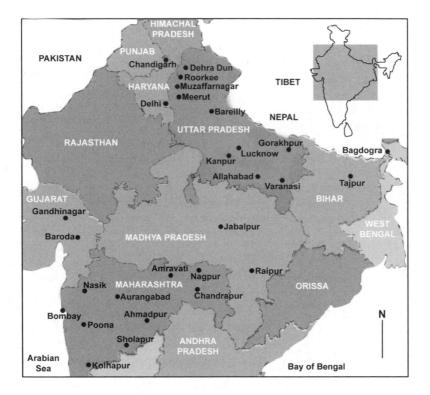

MAP OF INDIA: Places of Significance in *Joothan*

FOREWORD

Arun Prabha Mukherjee

OMPRAKASH VALMIKI'S *Joothan* is among the few books that have had a profound effect on my consciousness. It brought to the surface, as a scalpel penetrating deep into the flesh, the details of my childhood and adolescence in a small town in northern India where casteism and untouchability were normal, where untouchables cleaned our latrines and carried the excrement away on their heads. When they asked for water, it was poured into their cupped hands, from a distance. No untouchables studied with me in my school or later at college. My textbooks did inform me about the evil of untouchability and what Mahatma Gandhi had done to eliminate it, but they did so in a detached, abstracted manner, couched in a language that seemed to have no connection with my lived reality.

My Hindi literature textbook included a poem by Siaramsharan Gupt. This poem, entitled "Achut ki Aah" (The Sigh of an Untouchable), narrates the sad story of an untouchable denied entry into a temple and how it broke his heart. Such portrayals of Dalits (as untouchables are now called) as mute and pathetic characters, unable to act or speak about their oppression, are characteristic of high-caste Indian writers. They portray Dalits as tragic figures and objects of pity, incapable of talking back or feeling enraged. Arundhati Roy's *The God of Small Things* (1997), which won the Booker Prize in 1997, and Rohinton Mistry's *A Fine Balance* (1995) are also written in this appropriative voice, a voice that contains, rather than expresses, the Dalit experience.

Joothan had a visceral effect on me because in writing his life story of being born in the Chuhra caste and growing up in Barla in northern India, Valmiki spoke of the realities and contradictions of my society that thick walls of denial had shut out. Although I had been introduced to Marathi Dalit literature in translation before I read *Joothan*, its impact was much higher on the Richter scale of my consciousness because it was speaking of my corner of India, in my first language, Hindi, in a way that no other text had ever spoken to me.

I wanted to translate it the moment I finished reading it. I wanted to share this text with a wider readership in the hope that they too will feel its transformative power. I believe that here in *Joothan*, readers of English-language texts will find another answer to Gayatri Spivak's famous question: "Can the subaltern speak?"

Perhaps we need to ask another question: Can dominant society make space for the subaltern to speak? I have translated *Joothan* as my contribution to making that space. Hardly any Dalit literature is available in translation. High-caste and elite Indian voices, whether in India or in diaspora, continue to represent *the* Indian voice. It is time that this monopoly is ruptured and other voices heard.

Joothan is one among a body of Dalit writing that is unified by an ideology, an agenda, and a literary aesthetic. It provides an apt introduction to this newly emerging school of writing, which is not just a school of writing but sees itself as part of a social movement for equality and justice. As is shown by the list of authors that Valmiki enumerates in *Joothan*, Dalit writers have read and been inspired by the work of writers from many parts of the world.

It is time now that they be read in other parts of the world. I hope that the English translation of *Joothan* will enlarge Valmiki's readership many times.

In *Joothan* Valmiki writes: "We need an ongoing struggle and a consciousness of struggle, a consciousness that brings revolutionary change both in the outside world and in our hearts, a consciousness that leads the process of social change."

As a reader who believes in the important role that literature can play in the ongoing project of human liberation, I was inspired by these words, and I hope that others will be as well.

YORK UNIVERSITY
TORONTO

OMPRAKASH VALMIKI'S FAMILY TREE

Jaharia (great-grandfather)

Buddha (grandfather) — Kundan (great uncle)

Sugan Chand
Tau ji
married
(unnamed)
Tai ji

Chotan Lal
Pitaji
married
Mukundi
Mata ji

Molhar
Chacha ji
died, aged 22

Solhar
Chacha ji
(later lived with Ramkatori)

Shyamlal
Chacha ji
married
Ramkatori
(marriage broke up)

Chhoti
Bua ji

Shyamo
Bua ji

Sukhbir
died, aged 25
married
Rahti Devi
Bhabi ji

Jagdish
died, aged 18

(unnamed)
Mama ji

Jasbir
married
Rahti Devi
Bhabi ji

Janesar
married
Bimla Devi
Bhabi ji

Omprakash
b. 30 June 1950
married
Chandrakala
(younger sister
of Swarnalata,
Surjan's wife)

Maya
married

Soomti
died, aged 2

Sukhbir   **Jasbir**

Surjan
married
Swarnalata
Bhabi ji (elder sister of Chandrakala)

Sanjay   **Manju**

Seema   **Rajiv**   **Vinita**

PREFACE TO THE
HINDI EDITION

DALIT LIFE IS EXCRUCIATINGLY PAINFUL, charred by experiences. Experiences that did not manage to find room in literary creations. We have grown up in a social order that is extremely cruel and inhuman. And compassionless toward Dalits.

I have wanted to put the narrative of my pain into writing for a long time. But even though I tried many times, I did not succeed. I started to write umpteen times and ended up ripping the written pages apart. I could not decide where to begin or how. Some friends suggested that I should write a novel rather than an auto-biography.

Out of the blue came a letter from a publisher, Rajkishorji, in December 1993. He was planning a book called *Harijan se Dalit* (From Harijan to Dalit) in the *Aaj ke Prashn* (Questions for Today) series. He wanted me to write about ten or eleven pages in an autobiographical form for this anthology. Although I was free to change the names of the people involved, the experiences had to be true and verifiable. This letter caused me much turmoil.

For several days I could not decide what to do. I did not write a single sentence. And then a second letter arrived from Rajkishorji with an ultimatum: "Send your stuff by the end of January. The book is ready to go to press." I do not remember what else was in that letter, but that same night I sat down and wrote a few pages about my early life and posted them to Rajkishorji the next day. I waited a week for his reply and then rang him: he was going to publish those pages.

My essay, "Ek Dalit ki Atmakatha" (A Dalit's Autobiography), appeared on the very first pages of *Harijan se Dalit*. A stream of letters began to arrive for me as soon as the book came out. Responses came even from far-flung rural areas. Dalit readers had seen their own pain in those pages of mine. They all wanted me to write about my experiences in greater detail.

Putting these experiences on paper entailed all sorts of dangers. After a long period of procrastination I started to write. Once again I had to relive all those miseries, torments, neglects, admonitions. I suffered a deep mental anguish while writing this book. How terribly painful was this unraveling of my self, layer upon layer. Some people find this stuff unbelievable and exaggerated.

Many of my friends were astounded. Why was I writing an autobiography so early in my life? I beg to say to them: "Do not compare this narrative of pain with the achievements of others." A friend worried that I was eating away my literary capital by writing of my experiences autobiographically. Some others said that I would only contribute to the inferior status of my people by stripping myself naked. A close friend of mine fears that I will lose any prestige that I have if I write my autobiography.

Why should one feel awkward in telling the truth? To those who say that these things do not happen here, to those who want to claim a superior status for Indian civilization, I say that only those who have suffered this anguish know its sting.

Still, a lot remains unsaid. I did not manage to put it all down. It was beyond my power. You can call it my weakness.

The distinguished editor Rajendra Yadavji helped me a great deal in choosing the title. He found time in his busy life to read my manuscript and make suggestions. The title *Joothan* was his suggestion. Expressing my gratefulness to him is a mere formality. His guidance has been of tremendous value. Kanwal Bharti and Dr.

Shyoraj Singh Bechain provided me with emotional sustenance while I was writing this book. And, finally, I am grateful to Ashok Maheshwariji; without him this book would never have been completed. Just the interest that he showed in bringing it out solved many of my problems.

DEHRA DUN, 1997

OMPRAKASH VALMIKI

INTRODUCTION

Arun Prabha Mukherjee

OMPRAKASH VALMIKI'S *Joothan* is among the first texts in Hindi that identifies itself as a part of Dalit literature, one of the most important literary movements to emerge in postindependence India. On one level this is an autobiographical account of Valmiki's journey from his birth and upbringing as an untouchable in the newly independent India of the 1950s to today and his pride in being a Dalit. On another level *Joothan* is also a report card on the condition of people who are now routinely called "erstwhile untouchables" or "ex-untouchables."

Untouchability was legally abolished when the independent India adopted its constitution on November 26, 1949. Valmiki portrays a slice of life that had seldom been recorded in Indian literature until the advent of Dalit literature in Marathi, the language of the state of Maharashtra (its capital is Bombay), in the 1950s and its subsequent spread to many other languages, notably, Tamil, Telugu, Malayalam, Gujarati, Hindi, Punjabi, and English. Until then, literature had been the domain of high castes in India. Literary representations either ignored untouchables or portrayed them as victims in need of saviors, as objects without voice and agency.

Dalits constitute about 16 percent of India's population. For centuries they have been at the bottom of India's social pyramid, denied even the most basic human rights, such as access to drinking water from public ponds and wells, freedom to walk on public roads, and freedom to choose an occupation (they were assigned one at birth). The transformation of the stigma of untouchability through a self-chosen identity as a Dalit is a story of collective struggle waged over centuries.

The term *Dalit* forcefully expresses their oppressed status. It comes from the Sanskrit root *dal*, which means to crack open, split, crush, grind, and so forth, and it has generally been used as a verb to describe the process of processing food grains and lentils. Its metaphoric usage, still as a verb, is evident in descriptions of warfare and the vanquishing of enemies. Jotirao Phule and B. R. Ambedkar, two towering figures in Dalit history, were the first to appropriate the word, as a noun and an adjective, in the early decades of the twentieth century to describe the extreme oppression of untouchables.[1] The term *Dalit literature* was first used in 1958, at the first Dalit literature conference, which was held in Bombay. However, as an identity marker, *Dalit* came into prominence in 1972, when a group of young Marathi writer-activists founded an organization called the Dalit Panthers. The name expressed their feelings of solidarity and kinship with the Black Panthers, who were engaged in a militant struggle for African Americans' rights in the United States.

B. R. Ambedkar (1891–1956), also known affectionately as Babasaheb, or Father, to his followers, was a politician and lawyer and is considered the greatest leader of the untouchables. He received his doctoral degree from Columbia University in 1917. He was indeed much influenced by the U.S. Constitution, especially the

---

1. Jotirao Phule (1827–90), a pioneering social reformer, was born into a lower-caste family in Maharashtra. In 1873 he founded the Satyashodhak Samaj (Truth-Seeking Society) to fight for the rights of the lower castes and for women.

Fourteenth Amendment, and by Booker T. Washington. Ambedkar became the minister for law in independent India in 1948 and wrote the draft of what became the Constitution of India (1949). It established a program of reservation, a system of quotas that gave Dalits a foothold in educational institutions, government jobs, and representative government, much like the later U.S. program of affirmative action. Conflict with the government led Ambedkar to resign his post in September 1951.

The term *Dalit* found a ready acceptance among untouchable communities all over India. This was the first time that they had been able to choose their identity collectively, rather than be named by others. The names given by others, whether they were ancient names describing their untouchable status—such as Achut, Panchamas, Atishudras, Avarnas, Antyajas, Asparshyas, or Pariahs—or government-assigned bureaucratic designations such as Depressed Classes and Scheduled Castes, or the name bestowed by Gandhi with apparent goodwill, namely, Harijan (God's people), evoked pain and conflict. People who oppose the Dalit movement continue to use many of these terms today as jibes and pejoratives. Dalit is a political identity, as opposed to a caste name. It expresses Dalits' knowledge of themselves as oppressed people and signifies their resolve to demand liberation through a revolutionary transformation of the system that oppresses them. As Bishop A. C. Lal said in his address to the first Dalit Solidarity Conference, meeting in 1992 in the city of Nagpur, "The word Dalit is a beautiful word, because it transcends narrow national and sectarian frontiers. It is a beautiful word because it embraces the sufferings, frustrations, expectations and groanings of the entire cosmos" (Lal 1995:xiii).[2] Arjun Dangle, a leading Dalit writer and founder of the Dalit literary movement, says: "Dalit is not a caste but a realization and is related to the experiences, joys and sorrows, and struggles of those in the lowest stratum of socie-

---

2. Nagpur is a place of immense symbolic significance in Dalit history because that was where Ambedkar converted to Buddhism on October 14, 1956.

ty. It matures with a sociological point of view and is related to the principles of negativity, rebellion and loyalty to science, thus finally ending as revolutionary" (1992:264–65).

By identifying themselves as Dalits, writers like Valmiki are embracing an identity that was born in the historic struggle to dismantle the caste system, which was responsible for their untouchable status, and to rebuild society on the principles of human dignity, equality, and respect. Their identification of caste as a central question of their discourse underscores the dominance of the high-caste Hindu point of view in all walks of Indian life—literary expression, education, or political governance. High-caste Indian writers, both Hindu and non-Hindu (caste has infected all religions in India) who are published both in India and abroad as "representers" of Indian life, seldom deal with caste and caste oppression in their works. The dominant discourse of postcolonial and subaltern theories, which are often the frameworks that Western universities use to teach Indian literature, mostly Indian English literature, not only refuses to notice the high-caste status of these writers but presents them as resistant voices, representing the oppression of "the colonized." The situation is slightly different in India. Here mainstream critics and reviewers have responded to Dalit writers' stark portrayals of caste discrimination with a sense of disbelief and accusations of exaggeration. They have claimed that caste is no longer relevant, either because it has already disappeared or because it is in the process of disappearing. In their view, therefore, Dalit writers are writing about old news. These critics and reviewers have also declared Dalit writing to be lacking in literary merit.

However, before we discuss the literary aspects of Dalit writing or enter the world of a Dalit text, it is useful to discuss the long and complex history of the evolution of the caste system in India and the various struggles that were waged against it, because caste and caste-based oppression are the most important themes of Dalit writing. Quite pertinent here is the response of Prabhakar Mande, an eminent folklorist and distinguished scholar of Marathi drama, to critics who embrace the autonomy of the literary text: "The event of the development of Dalit literature is not just a literary event. Therefore this literature should not be viewed only from a literary perspective. Unless this literary chain of events is seen from a sociological perspective against the entire background of the changes happening in society, its significance will not be grasped" (Mande 1979, quoted in Limbale, in press).

From Untouchable to Dalit

Ambedkar himself declared that "the main cause which is responsible for the fate of the Untouchables is the Hindu religion and its teachings" (1989b:91). Although historians of ancient India have speculated on the origins of untouchability in the course of their larger surveys, and while modern sociologists have studied caste as a social phenomenon, there is, as Prabhati Mukherjee says, "some amount of hesitation and reluctance . . . among Indologists and historians to study the past history of the untouchables" (1988:12). Mukherjee is the only scholar besides Ambedkar to have done a book-length study of the origins of untouchability. Although Mukherjee's book is extremely illuminating, Ambedkar's comprehensive and eloquent work investigates the problem of untouchability from an insider's perspective and is therefore unique for its combination of historical, sociological, political, and experiential perspectives.

Little historical information of either a textual or archeological nature exists about the institutions of caste and untouchability. As Mukherjee says, "After a long and tedious wandering through the labyrinth of innumerable texts, one may find a word or a line about people not liked by that particular author" (1988:15). Many historians of ancient India echo her words of frustration about the lack of evidence. D. D. Kosambi, the pioneering historian of ancient India, answers Mukherjee's question of who is writing for whom: "Most surviving Sanskrit literature has been the creation of Brahmins or in their possession, or in some way stamped by brahminism" ([1975] 1995:101).

However, historians generally agree that the phenomena of caste and untouchability evolved over time, as a result of conflicts about land, resources, and cultural practices between a people who called themselves Aryans when they began arriving in India about the beginning of the second millennium B.C., and the various communities of indigenous people that ranged from citizens of highly developed city-states to forest-dwelling hunters and gatherers. In time these conflicts produced the *chaturvarna*, the system of society that categorizes all castes according to four major divisions, which were arranged hierarchically in a descending order of "purity." (The word *varna* literally means color, which refers to gradations within the hierarchy.) At the top of this power structure were the Brahmins, who were performers of rituals and keepers of sacred texts (the Vedas, the *Smritis*, and the *Puranas*), and the Kshatriyas, who, as rulers and warriors, patronized the Brahmins and commissioned the rituals, including the *yagna*, or fire ritual of animal sacrifices and gifts to Brahmins.[3] Although the Brahmins and Kshatriyas were constantly feuding for control of power, these two *varnas* considered themselves superior to the Vaisyas—the cultivators and traders—and the Sudras, the servants and performers of menial tasks. The Brahmins, in alliance with the king or state, denied the Sudras the ritual of *upanayana*, the sacred thread ceremony, which gave the three *varnas* above them the status of *dwija*, or twice born. Hindus must undergo this ritual, which symbolizes a second birth, before

---

3. The Vedas (*veda* means knowledge), which date to between the second and seventh centuries A.D., are considered the most sacred texts of Hinduism and were transmitted orally for centuries before being written down. The *Smritis* (*smriti* means remembered), also sacred texts but of a later period, stress the religious merits of giving gifts to Brahmins and lay down codes of behavior and law. The *Puranas* (*purana* means old), sacred texts of lesser importance from the fourth to eighth centuries A.D., relate myths, legends, and genealogies of the gods, heroes, and saints; they became the scriptures of the common people (Sudras and all women) because, unlike the Vedas, the *Puranas* were not restricted to initiated male Brahmins, Kshatriyas, and Vaisyas.

they may study the Vedas. Because the Sudras had no right to participate in this ritual, they were born only once, from the womb of a woman. Mukherjee speculates that the Aryans made strategic alliances with the autochthonous groups, and the friendly or powerful among them were incorporated into the *varna* system at the higher level. The Sudra category, on the other hand, "in all probability owes its origin to the non-wealthy, conquered and hostile groups" (Mukherjee 1988:24).

Mukherjee speculates further that as settled society, which was based on agriculture and industry, evolved in ancient India, the four-division *varna* system was further divided by a *jati*, or caste-based division; a caste was a group whose membership came with birth and maintained its separation by practicing endogamy and commensalism, that is, marrying and eating only with members of one's own caste. The caste system, she suggests, allowed for a more closely knit social organization that permitted privileged groups to maintain their exclusiveness more stringently than in the four large divisions of the *varna* system. The number of castes, and stratification among them, increased as the *varna* system incorporated more and more newcomers.

Although the doctrine of *chaturvarna* accounts for the beginning of the process by which the four *varnas* gradually proliferated into modern-day castes, Ambedkar points out that it does not explain untouchability and the branding of certain castes as untouchable. He theorizes that untouchability began after the great struggle for supremacy between the Brahmins and the Buddhists. According to him, Brahmins began practicing untouchability against beef eaters after the Brahmins stopped sacrificing cows and eating beef in order to win an ideological battle against the Buddhists. The latter were preaching against *yagnas* and animal sacrifice, thereby winning over the cultivators and traders, who were greatly inconvenienced when Brahmins and Kshatriyas seized their cattle for ritual sacrifices without payment, as their entitlement. Ambedkar speculates that in order to regain the allegiance of the trading and farming classes, the Brahmins not only gave up animal sacrifices but went one step further than the Buddhists and banned the killing of cows and the eating of flesh altogether.

The Gupta kings banned cow slaughter some time in the fourth century A.D. However, according to Ambedkar, certain sections of the society continued to eat beef. These beef eaters were outside the four-*varna* system. They lived outside the villages settled by the *savarnas*, that is, those *within* the *varna* system. Theoretically, the beef eaters were not violating the laws against cow slaughter because they ate the flesh of cows that had died of natural causes; the beef eaters' job was to remove dead cows as a service to the *savarna* villagers. Ambedkar calls these people "broken men." He believes that they were the remnants of conquered and fragmented tribes that settled outside the *savarna* villages and survived by performing the most degrading tasks for the *savarnas*. These people were called *avarnas* because they were *outside* the *varna* system, and they were untouchable because of their association with carrion and other polluting substances.

Mukherjee suggests that the Aryans punished groups hostile to them by declaring them ritually impure and by keeping them outside the villages and towns:"One touching a *chandala* [untouchable] ... should bathe with one's clothes on. ... To touch, talk with or even to look at a *chandala* made one undergo penance. ... For touching an Aryan woman a *chandala* was fined one hundred panas, and for adultery with her a *shavapaca* [untouchable] was sentenced to death (1988:41)." And further:"The *chandalas* were the lowest and the worst of all human beings. ... Strong hatred for them is expressed not only by the *Brahmanas* but in the *Jatakas* as well.[4] For instance, the sight of *chandala* was inauspicious, ... and

---

4. The *Brahmanas* (ca. 1500–1000 B.C.) are ritual texts in Sanskrit that were created after the Vedas, giving details of the sacrifices and also indicating changes in the hierarchy of gods. Prominent in these texts is the word *brahman*, which refers to the creative power of the ritual utterances and the sacrifice, which in turn underlies ritual and therefore cosmic power. The *Jatakas*, of which there are about six hundred, are part of Buddhist literature and focus on the incarnations of the Buddha before he attained Buddhahood. They too are a valuable historical source.

daughters of a *shresthi* [merchant] and priest washed their eyes after having accidentally seen a *chandala* because he was not fit to be seen" (63).

Ambedkar thinks that untouchability was born around 400 A.D.: "It is born out of the struggle for supremacy between Buddhism and Brahminism which has so completely moulded the history of India and the study of which is so woefully neglected by students of Indian history" (1990:379).

One may agree or disagree with Ambedkar's hypotheses regarding the origins of caste and untouchability; however, untouchables have long lived outside the village boundaries, subsisting on the flesh of dead draft animals that they had the duty to dispose of. During the independence movement many a leader of the Indian National Congress, the main nationalist political party, gave the consumption of carrion by untouchables as the reason that caste Hindus (as high-caste Hindus were then called; untouchables were called outcastes) practiced untouchability. Although Ambedkar also advised his followers to give up eating carrion, he replied to the caste Hindus that untouchables had resorted to eating it only because they were too poor to get anything else and not because they loved it.

Whether the untouchables are Hindus became a highly sensitive issue during the early years of the twentieth century when leaders of the Indian National Congress were demanding home rule from the British colonial government, and matters of proportional representation for Hindus and Muslims came to the forefront. Muslim leaders submitted a petition to the British government that claimed that untouchables, as outcastes, were not a part of the Hindu population. Ambedkar, along with other leaders of the untouchables, demanded separate electorates for untouchables.[5] He argued that untouchables were not Hindus because they were not included in the *chaturvarna* system. For him,

---

5. These separate electorates are the equivalents of voting districts wherein only untouchable or Dalit candidates can be elected. Even non-Dalit voters must vote for Dalit candidates to ensure a Dalit presence in Parliament.

Gandhi's claim that untouchables were an indivisible part of "the Hindu fold" was merely expedient. He saw it as a ploy to allow caste Hindus to grab political power and continue to keep untouchables under their foot.

Gandhi went on a fast unto death after the British colonial government of India announced its intention to grant separate electorates to the untouchables. He got his way. Ambedkar, forced to withdraw his demand, signed the so-called Poona Pact of 1932. Indian history textbooks today rarely mention his capitulation under pressure. However, Dalits see the pact that killed their demand for separate electorates as a great betrayal. (Independent India's Constitution, which Ambedkar shaped to a considerable extent, declares its support for a more egalitarian society and permits separate electorates, which are "reserved" for Dalits.) Dalit literature memorializes the idea of separate electorates in a variety of symbolic and thematic ways.

Whether Dalits are Hindu remains a burning question to this day. At a mammoth meeting in 1935 Ambedkar had declared that although he was born a Hindu, he was not going to die as one. True to his word, he embraced Buddhism on October 14, 1956, along with millions of his followers, just three months before his death. Since then, Dalits have participated in many mass conversions. High-caste Hindu forces have tried to prevent these through various means. Kancha Ilaiah's *Why I Am Not a Hindu* (1996) eloquently contests today's dominant Hindutva forces (right-wing Hindu demand for Hindu political domination), which want to project a unitary Hindu identity based on Vedic principles. Dalit writers, including Valmiki, satirize this celebration of "ancient glory" because it valorizes the very texts that sanctioned the unjust and inhuman treatment of the Sudras and the untouchables. Ambedkar's attitude and actions vis-à-vis these ancient texts influence Dalit writers and leaders. In a famous but undelivered 1936 speech, later printed as "Annihilation of Caste," Ambedkar proclaimed: "You have got to apply the dynamite to the Vedas and the Shastras [the body of sacred literature of the

Hindus] which deny any part to reason" ([1979] 1989a:75). And nine years earlier, on December 25, 1927, while leading the famous agitation to gain Dalits the right to draw water from Chavdar Lake at Mahad, Maharashtra, Ambedkar had, in a powerfully symbolic act, burned the *Manusmriti* (The Laws of Manu) in a bonfire. Ambedkar decided to burn this text because its author, Manu, is the ancient sage credited with codifying the brahminical laws of untouchability and pollution.

The ideological differences between Dalits and caste Hindus in regard to the Vedas and other sacerdotal texts, *chaturvarna*, and the caste system caused a deep rift between the Dalits and the leadership of the Indian National Congress, which was dominated by high-caste Hindus and derided by Ambedkar as a "bourgeois-Brahmin" organization. Gandhi, for example, believed that the caste system and untouchability were distortions that could be purged from Hinduism without discarding *chaturvarna*, which he believed to be a unique gift of India to world civilization. He felt that untouchables must not stop performing their hereditary functions because that is what the *varna* system asks of every Hindu. Writing in *Harijan* on March 6, 1937, Gandhi said:

> What I mean is, one born a scavenger must earn his livelihood by being a scavenger, and then do whatever else he likes. For a scavenger is as worthy of his hire as a lawyer or your president. That according to me is Hinduism. There is no better Communism on earth. Varnashram Dharma [the duties/moral code of the four varnas] acts even as the law of gravitation. The law of Varna is the antithesis of competition which kills.

Ambedkar differed radically from Gandhi on the question of reforming Hinduism. He declared that when Gandhi tried to salvage the *varna* system by saying that it had nothing to do with the caste system, he was simply quibbling, that the two were indeed symbiotically connected. Whereas Gandhi believed in the removal of untouchability through penance and acts of social service by caste Hindus, as opposed to mandated changes in the law, Ambedkar used the language of rights and legislated remedies. Similarly, while Gandhi and the other leaders of the Indian National Congress thought in terms of temple entry (forbidden to untouchables in the belief that their presence would pollute the temple) and "interdining," Ambedkar linked untouchability to the economic destitution of the untouchables, constantly reiterating how they were denied access to education, ownership of land, and jobs above the level of scavenging, picking up garbage, cleaning latrines, and other menial occupations. He repeatedly pointed out how, besides being denied access to avenues for economic better-ment, untouchables were forced to provide their labor against their will and without any control of their wages. In the words of Gail Omvedt, "The point is that Gandhi, who feared a 'political division . . . in the villages,' ignored the division that already existed; in his warning against the spread of violence, he ignored the violence already existing in the lives of the Dalits" (1994:172).

As Dalits waged battles for equality and dignity, the names that their oppressors had given them became an issue. So stigma-tized were untouchable caste names (I remember that my brother and I called each other "Chuhra" and "Chamar," the names of untouchable castes, during our childhood quarrels) that the Dalits wanted to discard these terms. The new names asserted the Dalits' claims that they were outside the *chaturvarna* and, indeed, were the aboriginal people of India. They adopted names like Adi-Dravida, Adi-Andhra, Adi-Hindu, and Adi-Karnataka to lay claim to an aboriginal identity (the word *adi* means "from the beginning"). This claiming of aboriginal status and a non-Aryan identity flies in the face of the Hindutva ideologues who see the Vedas, the texts of the Aryans, as the source of India's civilization and who claim that the Aryans did not come from central Asia but were indige-nous to India.

"Valmiki," or "Balmiki," was widely adopted as a caste name by the Chuhras of Punjab and western Uttar Pradesh under the influence of the Arya Samaj, a Hindu reform movement in northern India. Arya Samajists were alarmed by the conversion of large numbers of Chuhras to Christianity and Sikhism in the 1920s and the 1930s. The Arya Samajists started emulating the Christian missionaries by opening schools and hospitals for the untouchables and performing *shuddhi*, a purification ceremony to reconvert the Christian converts. Arya Samajists told Chuhras that they were the descendants of Valmiki, the creator of the Sanskrit epic *Ramayana*. Bhagwan Das suggests that caste Hindus appropriated the Chuhras' patron saint Lal Beg, or Bala Shah, and renamed him Valmiki in order to "Hinduize" themselves (Das n.d.:193). In *Joothan* Omprakash Valmiki relates how a Christian convert, Sewak Ram Masihi, came to his locality to teach the Chuhra children the alphabet. Valmiki's growing estrangement from Chuhra rituals made his father worry that his son might have converted to Christianity. When Valmiki's father finds out that his son has begun to use "Valmiki" as his surname, a sign of his self-pride, the older man is ecstatic.

Valmiki devotes several pages to the ironies that his new identity entails. While in Bombay, he is taken to be a Brahmin by a Maharashtrian Brahmin family, indicating the possibility of "passing" if one travels far enough from the place of one's birth. In western Uttar Pradesh, however, this surname does not lift the author up from his Chuhrahood and the attendant untouchability. The Buddhists see him as a casteist, a supporter of the caste system, because he refuses to shed this identity marker as a badge of self-assertion, a declaration that he does not want to hide his Dalit identity. Valmiki points out the daily dilemmas that Dalits face in a caste-based society that make it almost impossible to shed the caste marker and leave behind the stigmas attached to it.

In addition to the terminology that the Dalits chose, the government gave them bureaucratic nomenclatures. The term *Depressed Classes*, first used by missionaries in southern India, was later adopted by the British government in its official records. Ambedkar found the term "degrading and contemptuous" and suggested several alternatives for it, such as "noncaste Hindus,"

"Protestant Hindus," "nonconformist Hindus," "Excluded Castes," and "Exterior Castes." Nevertheless, in his own writings and speeches he continued to use *Depressed Classes* and *untouchables* interchangeably.

Gandhi replaced the term *untouchable* with *Harijan*. He claimed that "several untouchable correspondents" who had complained about his use of the term *asprishya* suggested the alternative to him. He explained in *Harijan* of February 11, 1933: "'Asprishya' means literally untouchable. I then invited them to suggest a better name, and one of the 'untouchable' correspondents suggested the adoption of the name 'Harijan,' on the strength of its having been used by [the] first known Poet-Saint of Gujarat."

Gandhi popularized the term *Harijan*, and the Government of India, bureaucrats, political leaders, and the national press later adopted it. Dalits, on the other hand, found it patronizing and infantilizing. Because of their vociferous protests, it has now generally gone out of favor.

A bureaucratic term that has stuck is *Scheduled Castes*. It refers to a list of untouchable castes that was prepared by the British government in 1935 and attached to the Order-in-Council issued under the Government of India Act of 1935. The Constitution of India uses Scheduled Castes in a more flexible way, leaving the making of the list, and deletions and additions to it, up to the government. The Scheduled Caste identity is a bureaucratic necessity for Dalits when they apply for reserved positions, which are often derided by anti-Dalits as quotas, and for other government benefits. The term usually is shortened to SC, and many high-caste Hindus associate it with favoritism, unequal treatment, pork-barrel politics, and giving educational and employment opportunities to people lacking in merit and qualifications, as when high-caste Hindus complain about the SCs taking away all the jobs. In *Joothan* Valmiki draws attention to the bitterness and ambivalence that Dalits feel when they must use the SC identity in order to be considered for jobs reserved for them by law and when others thrust it upon them in contempt.

Dalitbahujan is a new term, proposed by Kancha Ilaiah, who, like many other Dalit writers and activists, thinks that the term *Dalit* should not describe the status and situation of untouchables alone but should cover all victims of poverty and exploitation. The term means the majority and was first used by the founder of the Bahujan Samaj Party, Kanshi Ram, a Dalit from Punjab. Kanshi Ram, an Ambedkarite, proposed in the early 1980s that the untouchables, the Sudras (now given the bureaucratic name of Other Backward Classes—the word *classes* was thought to be more neutral than *castes*—usually abbreviated as OBCs), and other non-Hindu minorities, including the Scheduled Tribes (STs), together were more numerous than any single caste or ethnic group. If they united, they could become a political power. The Bahujan Samaj Party (BSP) was launched on April 14, 1984, Ambedkar's birthday. The party has been able to reduce the supremacy of Brahmins and Kshatriyas in Uttar Pradesh, the most populous province in India, where it is back in power for the fourth time. A measure of the complexity and oddity of identity politics in India today is that the party, which has made opportunistic alliances with the Hindu fundamentalist, or right-wing, party, the Bharatiya Janata Party, bagged an absolute majority in the 2007 elections with the support of the Brahmins.

Dalits are thus a major force in India today, playing a decisive role in shaping the future. Spread over the entire country, speaking many languages, and belonging to many religions, they are certainly not a homogeneous community. However, they continue to face certain problems, which emanate from their status as untouchables. The Dalit scholar Bhagwan Das provides a comprehensive snapshot of how untouchability affects the day-to-day lives of Dalits today:

> Land-holding upper caste people in villages do not allow the Dalits to wear decent clothes, cast votes freely, ride on a horse in marriage procession, draw water from a public

well, sit on a cot while the upper caste man is standing. In cities a student belonging to Scheduled Castes is purposely given low marks, an officer is prejudged as incompetent and inefficient just because of his birth in an untouchable caste. A professor, a lawyer, a doctor, an architect, born in an untouchable family, is considered inefficient and inferior without even seeing his performance. A patient refuses to be treated by a Scheduled Caste doctor and a house owner refuses to let a vacant house to him for the fear of pollution. A superior gives bad reports to a Dalit subordinate in order to obstruct his promotion. In everyday talk in the canteens, buses, trains and airplanes, offices and establishments, aspersions are cast on the men and women of untouchable origin and derogatory remarks are passed. Universities and colleges abusing the power and authority given to "autonomous bodies" close the doors of progress to students, teachers and employees to protect "merit"—merit earned with fake certificates, unfair practices in examination, nepotism and corruption. (1995:58)

Das's words portray only the day-to-day "normal" experiences of discrimination that Dalits undergo. In rural areas Dalits continue to face physical violence, including mass killings and rapes by vigilante groups established and operated by high-caste landowners, when Dalits ask for fair wages and freedom from molestation. The authorities seldom apprehend and punish the perpetrators of such violence. Dalits struggle against these injustices through political as well as cultural means. Dalit literature is one of the major sites of their resistance and creativity.

Dalit Literature and Dalit Literary Theory

Many Dalit writers have claimed a unique status for Dalit literature, in response to established literary critics who want to subsume it under wider categories of literature in different Indian languages and judge it according to criteria that they claim to be timeless and universal. As a rule, these judgments have been negative and even hostile. Dalit literary theory has emerged as a reaction to these critics. Sharankumar Limbale has summarized the objections that the so-called mainstream literary critics have raised about Dalit literature: "It has been charged that Dalit literature is propagandistic, univocal and negative; that it does not represent the individual person; and that excessive resentment is heard in Dalit literature" (2004:34).[6] Dalit writers have responded that Dalit literature appears to be propagandistic because it has emerged as part of the movement for Dalit liberation and its raison d'être remains the commitment to this movement. In his own book in Hindi on Dalit aesthetics Valmiki writes: "The Dalit literary movement is not just a literary movement. It is also a cultural and social movement. Dalit society has been imprisoned for a thousand years in the dark mist of ignorance, deprived of knowledge. Dalit literature is the portrayal of the wishes and aspirations of these oppressed and tormented Dalits" (2001:97).[7] Limbale reiterates this sentiment by saying that "because Dalit writers have presented their anguish and their questions in their literature, their literature has acquired a propagandistic character" (2004:35).

Dalit writers turn the tables on mainstream literary values by charging that the literature of the dominant group is not "good" literature because it has ignored the suffering and exploitation of Dalits. Stating that high-caste Marathi literature is artificial and false, like a paper flower, M. N. Wankhade adds that "a Marathi writer's understanding of life is restricted. . . . He has never seen that outside there is a vast world—a suffering, distressed, strug-

---

6. All quotations from Sharankumar Limbale, *Towards an Aesthetic of Dalit Literature: History, Controversies, and Considerations*, translated by Alok Mukherjee (Hyderabad, India: Orient Longman, 2004). I am thankful to the translator for giving me access to the manuscript before publication.

7. This and all subsequent translations of the Hindi edition of Omprakash Valmiki, *Dalit Sahitya ka Saundaryashastra* (Delhi: Radhakrishna, 2001), are mine.

gling, howling world, burning with anger from within like a prairie fire" (1992:316).

Valmiki finds similar problems of caste and class bias in contemporary Hindi literature and says that since upper-caste writers do not know the miseries of Dalits, what they write remains superficial, born out of sympathy but not out of a desire for change or repentance. Dalit writers and critics have contested attempts by mainstream critics to include these high-caste portrayals of Dalits under the rubric of Dalit literature. They claim that Dalit literature can be written only by Dalits: "Removing and cutting dead animals—how will non-Dalits write about this experience of Dalits with the power of their imagination? How will they feel the angry ideas rising in the hearts of untouchables on the basis of their helpless imagination?" (2004:104). In a similar vein Valmiki ridicules the Hindi writer Kashinath Singh, who said that "one does not have to be a horse in order to write about one. . . . Only the horse, tethered to its stall after a whole day's exhausting labor, knows how it feels, and not its owner" (2001:x). In making such claims, Dalit writers are not alone; aboriginal writers in the United States and Canada have made similar declarations.

This battle about representation is reminiscent of the struggle between Gandhi and Ambedkar in 1932. At the roundtable conference held in London to discuss the future of India, Gandhi denied Ambedkar's claim to be the representative of untouchables, and Gandhi claimed for himself the identity of a "self-chosen untouchable." Dalit writers demand that their right to self-represent be acknowledged. However, not only has this right been constantly challenged but Dalit writers' representations have also been denounced as false. Every time a Dalit writer's story is published in the Hindi monthly publication *Hans*, the editor receives a flurry of letters claiming that the atrocities described in the story are untrue.

Clearly, readers are strongly divided about the value of Dalit literature, and Dalit writers have decided to depend on their own value judgments. According to Limbale, "The standard of a work of literature depends on how much and in what way an artist's ideas embedded in the work affect the reader. . . . 'That work of Dalit literature will be recognized as beautiful, and, therefore, 'good' which causes the greatest awakening of 'Dalit consciousness in the reader'" (2004:117).

Responding to those who find Dalit literature lacking in aesthetic sophistication, Limbale declares that "Freedom is the [highest] aesthetic value. . . . Equality, freedom, justice and love are basic sentiments of people and society. They are many times more important than pleasure and beauty" (2004:117).

Thus what detractors have enumerated as faults, Dalit writers have embraced as the distinct aspects of Dalit aesthetics. Defining Dalit literature and its characteristics substantively, Valmiki says, "Dalit literature is the literature of the masses. It is a literature of action, based on human values, which wages a struggle born out of anger and rebellion against feudalistic mindsets" (2001:15).

There are many points of conjuncture between Marxist and Dalit perspectives on the world, society, and literature. Theorists like Limbale feel that Dalit literature and literary theory should not reject Marxism just because Indian Marxists have completely ignored caste-based oppression, forgetting the truth of Ambedkar's observation that caste creates a division of workers. Nevertheless, many Dalit writers harbor considerable suspicion vis-à-vis Marxist theory and Indian Marxists. Ilaiah says that Marxism in India lost its revolutionary edge because it "fell into the hands of most reactionary forces—the Brahmins, the Baniyas [traders and merchants, i.e., the Vaisyas] and the neo-Kshatriyas" (1996:50). Omvedt says that "Indian leftists have not paid adequate attention to cultural and symbolic issues. They have thus not confronted the meaning and forms of the brahminic hegemonising of Indian culture" (1996:vii–viii).

Dalit Literature and Autobiography

Autobiography has been a favorite genre of Dalit writers. This is not surprising, in light of the emphasis that they place on authenticity of experience. Here again Dalit writers have faced criticism

from mainstream critics who say that autobiography is not a literary genre. Moreover, they have claimed that Dalit autobiographies
are unstructured, artless outpourings of Dalit writers' unmediated
experience and have become repetitive and stereotypical. Valmiki
says that even some Dalit writers have internalized this negative
view of autobiography. Valmiki quotes Das's defense of the genre:
"'Dalit writers should write autobiographies so that not only our
history will stay alive but also our true portrayals of wrongdoers.
Dalit autobiographies will provide inspiration to our future gener-
ations'" (Valmiki 2001:20).

Valmiki and other Dalit writers thus interrogate the mainstream critics' allocation of a nonliterary status to autobiography.
Ilaiah says that a narrative of "personal experience brings out
reality in a striking way. . . . Ambedkar and Periyar spoke and
wrote on the day-to-day experiences of the Dalitbahujan castes.[8]
I would argue that this is the only possible and indeed the most
authentic way in which the deconstruction and reconstruction of
history can take place" (1996:xii). Answering mainstream critics,
Valmiki says that autobiography is not just a remembering of
things past but a shaping and structuring of them in such a way
as to help understand one's life and the social order that shaped
it, on the one hand, and to arouse a passion for change in the
Dalit reader on the other.

One main point of Dalit literary analysis is that Dalit literature is based on real life and the lived experience of Dalit writers.
While mainstream critics have seen this as evidence of a lack of
imagination in Dalit writing, suggesting that Dalit literature is
nothing but reportage, Dalit writers point to the authenticity of
experience as the most important characteristic of Dalit writing.

---

8. *Periyar* means great soul, or mahatma, the honorific given to E. P. Ramasamy
Naicker (1880–1974), the great leader of the non-Brahmins of Tamil Nadu. Naicker
founded the Dravida Kazhagam, or Dravidian Federation, a party of political, social,
and cultural reform that rallied south Indians against the Brahmin hegemony and
called on them to take pride in their own distinct culture. He founded the Self-
Respect movement for non-Brahmins.

Reading Valmiki's short story collection, *Salaam*, for example, one is struck by how many stories are based on the life experiences that Valmiki describes in *Joothan*. When I questioned him about it during an interview, Valmiki insisted that all his stories are based on real incidents.[9]

Another important credo of Dalit writing is the rejection of Hindu mythology as anti-Dalit and brahminist. According to Dangle, "The tradition and culture of ancient India do not contain anything which a Dalit can own with pride" (1992:264). Dalit analyses of ancient Indian sacerdotal texts have been irreverent, turning the heroes into villains and vice versa. Ilaiah retells the mythological stories about gods and goddesses like Ram and Sita, Shiva and Parvati, Vishnu and Lakshmi, and others from a Dalit point of view, rehabilitating the traditionally demonized characters in them. He says: "All the Gods and Goddesses are institutionalized, modified and contextualized in a most brazen anti-Dalitbahujan mode. Hinduism has been claiming that the Dalitbahujans are Hindus, but at the same time their very Gods are openly against them" (1992:72).

Valmiki says that Dalit literature has recuperated such stigmatized characters as Eklavya, Karna, and Shambuk from ancient epics and established them as heroes (2001:87). How consciously Dalit writers use language became evident to me when, during our interview, Valmiki explained that he used the analogy of the goddess Durga in *Joothan* to describe his mother's anger when she throws away the basketful of *joothan* after the higher-caste character Sukhdev Singh Tyagi insults her. This is the only place in the text where he draws on traditional Hindu mythology. Like the goddess, who is the embodiment of *shakti* or power, his mother will not be submissive against such an insult but will avenge herself. Valmiki said that he used the analogy under duress, because he could not find another equivalent that would appropriately describe his mother's heroic action and her

---

9. I interviewed Omprakash Valmiki in Dehra Dun on July 4, 2002.

anger. (The goddess Durga is the protective mother who will also use her power to rid the world of evil.)

Dalit writers like Valmiki are thus producing literary analysis and literary theory simultaneously with their literary creations. They show tremendous independence of mind when they reevaluate canonical literature, respond to conservative critics who talk about "literary standards," and analyze Dalit writings from a Dalit-centric perspective. The high-caste literary establishment can no longer continue to present its choices as universal and timeless. Moreover, by producing their own discourse and publishing it in small Dalit-run journals, Dalit writers have created a space for themselves.

Joothan: A Dalit Literary Text

In his preface Valmiki writes that *Joothan* presents "experiences that did not find room in literary creations." Experiences like Valmiki's—his birth and growing up in the untouchable caste of Chuhra, the bottom slot preassigned to him because of this accident of birth, the heroic struggle that he waged to survive this preordained life of perpetual physical and mental persecution, his coming to consciousness under the influence of Ambedkarite thought, and his transformation into a speaking subject and recorder of the oppression and exploitation that he endured not only as an individual but as a member of a stigmatized and oppressed community—had never been represented in the annals of Hindi literature. He therefore has broken new ground, mapped a new territory. Besides a few stray poems and short stories by canonical Hindi writers, which portray Dalit characters as tragic figures and objects of pathos, Dalit representations are conspicuously absent from contemporary Hindi literature.

A literary critic, reared in an educational system that taught a canon of literature focused solely on the experience of the privileged sections of society, whether of India or of the West, must

tread cautiously in this new territory, using the benchmarks provided by Dalit literary theory and continuously on guard against
those kinds of formalist analyses that privilege form over content.

How far removed Valmiki's subject matter is from the day-to-
day experience of an urban middle-class reader is evident from the
very title, *Joothan*. It proves the truth of Dangle's claim that Dalit
writing demands a new dictionary, for the words that it uses are as
new as the objects, situations, and activities that they describe
(1992:252). The Hindi word *joothan* literally means food left on a
plate, usually destined for the garbage pail in a middle-class urban
home. However, such food would be characterized *joothan* only if
someone else were to eat it. The word carries the connotations of
ritual purity and pollution, because *jootha* means polluted. I feel
that words such as *leftovers* or *leavings* are not adequate substitutes
for *joothan*. *Leftovers* has no negative connotations and can simply
mean food remaining in the pot that can be eaten at the next meal;
leavings, although widely used by Ambedkar and Gandhi, is no
longer in the active vocabulary of Indian English. *Scraps* and *slops*
are somewhat closer to *joothan*, but they are associated more with
pigs than with humans.

The title encapsulates the pain, humiliation, and poverty of
Valmiki's community, which not only had to rely on *joothan* but
also relished it. Valmiki gives a detailed description of collecting,
preserving, and eating *joothan*. His memories of being assigned to
guard the drying *joothan* from crows and chickens, and of his rel-
ishing the dried and reprocessed *joothan*, burn him with renewed
pain and humiliation many years later. The term actually carries a
lot of historical baggage. Both Ambedkar and Gandhi advised
untouchables to stop accepting *joothan*. Ambedkar, an indefatiga-
ble documenter of atrocities against Dalits, shows how the high-
caste villagers could not tolerate the decision of Dalits to no longer
accept *joothan* and threatened Dalits with violence if they refused
it. Valmiki has thus recovered a word from the painful past of
Dalit history, and it resonates with multiple ironies. Gandhi's
paternalistic preaching, which assumed that accepting *joothan* was

simply a bad habit that the untouchables could discard, when juxtaposed with Ambedkar's passionate exhortation to fellow untouchables to not accept *joothan* even when its refusal provoked violence, press against Valmiki's text, proliferating in multiple meanings.

It is not surprising, therefore, that one of the most powerful moments of the text comes when Valmiki's mother overturns a basketful of *joothan* after Sukhdev Singh Tyagi humiliates her. Her act of defiance is an example of rebellion to the child Valmiki. He has dedicated the book to her and his father and portrays both as heroic figures who desired something better for their child and fought for his safety and growth with tremendous courage. His father's ambitions for his son are evident in the nickname that he gave him, Munshiji. An honorific title, it meant an officer who kept and prepared records. The child Valmiki rises on their shoulders to become the first high school graduate from his neighborhood. He pays his debt by giving voice to the indignities suffered by his parents and other Dalits.

Valmiki's inscription of these moments of profound violation of his and his people's human rights is extremely powerful and deeply disturbing. He constructs *Joothan* in the form of wave upon wave of memories that erupt in his mind when triggered by a stimulus in the present. These are memories of trauma that Valmiki had suppressed. He uses the metaphors of erupting lava, explosions, conflagrations, and flooding to denote their uncontrollable character. The text follows the logic of the recall of these memories. Instead of following a linear pattern, Valmiki moves from memory to memory, showing how his present is deeply scarred by his past despite the great distance that he has traveled to get away from it. The text abounds in metaphors of assault, wound, dismemberment, scarring, and so on, conveying the brutality and violence of the social order that the narrator inhabits.

Valmiki presents the traumatic moments of encounter with his persecutors as dramatized scenes, as cinematic moments. His narration of the event captures the intensity of the memory and suggests that he has not yet healed from these traumas of the past. We see a full-dress reenactment of the event from the perspective of the child or the adolescent Valmiki. Many Dalit texts share this strategy of staging encounters between the Dalit narrator and people of upper castes. Often these encounters are between a Dalit child at his or her most vulnerable and an upper-caste adult in a position of authority. The fullness of detail with which they are inscribed suggests how strongly these past events are imprinted in the narrator's mind.

The Dalit narrator lives these traumatic experiences again but this time in order to go past them by understanding them in an ethical framework and passing judgment on them, something that the child could not do. Valmiki thus provides a double exposure, first capturing the event from the perspective of a traumatized child and the fear and danger that he experienced and then layering it with the adult narrator's perspective, condemning the social system that allowed the perpetrators of such atrocities to go unpunished. The theoretical glossing of the experience, then, is a sort of healing, a symbol of having overcome it by naming it and sharing it with a caring community.

By documenting these experiences of the Dalit child, first by theatricalizing them so that we see them for ourselves and then by commenting on them in the ethical language of guilt and responsibility from the perspective of the victim, Valmiki and other Dalit writers break through the wall of silence and denial that had hidden the suffering of the Dalits. Valmiki's encounters with his various schoolteachers show how Dalit children are abused verbally, physically, and publicly, without anyone coming to their rescue. He relives the agony of having to sit away from his classmates, on the floor, of being denied the right to drink from the common pitcher, lest he make it *jootha*, and, worst of all, being denied access to the lab, which ensured his failure in an examination. The text, as testimony to a crime suffered, acquires the character of a victim impact statement.

Valmiki intertextualizes his and his Dalit friends' encounters with upper-caste teachers and the Brahmin teacher Dronacharya in the *Mahabharata*. Dronacharya tricked his low-caste disciple Eklavya into amputating his thumb and presenting it as part of his *gurudakshina*, or teacher's tribute.[10] By doing this, Dronacharya ensured that Eklavya, the better student of archery, could never compete against Arjun, the Kshatriya disciple. Indeed, after losing his thumb, Eklavya could no longer perform archery. When people of high caste tell this popular story, they present a casteless Eklavya as the exemplar of an obedient disciple rather than the Brahmin Dronacharya as a perfidious and biased teacher. When Valmiki's father goes to the school and calls the headmaster a Dronacharya, he links twentieth-century caste relations to those that prevailed two thousand years ago. By showing his father's ability to deconstruct the story, Valmiki portrays Dalits as articulate subjects who have seen through the cherished myths of their oppressors. When in a literature class a teacher waxes eloquent about this same Dronacharya, Valmiki challenges the teacher, only to be ruthlessly caned. Valmiki's reconfiguration of the myth also intertextualizes *Joothan* with other Dalit texts, which frequently use the character of Eklavya as representing the denial of education to Dalits. The modern Dalit Eklavya, however, can no longer be tricked into self-mutilation.

While Valmiki indicts the education system as dealing in death for Dalits, Valmiki pays tribute to the Dalit organic intellectuals who help nurture the growth of a Dalit consciousness in him. Although one of these is his father, who has the temerity to call the headmaster a Dronacharya, another is Chandrika Prasad Jigyasu, whose rendering of Ambedkar's life is put into Valmiki's hands by his friend Hemlal. Hemlal has shed his stigmatized identity as a Chamar by changing his name from Jatia, which identifies him as an untouchable, to Jatav, which is not readily identifiable.[11] Reading

---

10 The *Mahabharata* is a classical Sanskrit epic composed between 200 B.C. and 200 A.D.

11. See page 79.

about Ambedkar's life is a transformative moment for Valmiki, rendered in the metaphors of melting away his deadening silence and the magical transformation of his muteness into voice. This moment, narrativized at length in *Joothan*, gives us a key to how marginalized groups walk onto the stage of history. Valmiki underscores the way that Ambedkar has been excised from the hagiography of nationalist discourse. Valmiki first encounters Ambedkar through the writing of a fellow Dalit, passed on to him by another Dalit, in a library run by Dalits. When I interviewed Valmiki, he told me that Chandrika Prasad Jigyasu used to publish inexpensive and accessible materials on Ambedkar's life and bought and sold these publications on the street himself. Valmiki says that he emulated Jigyasu and sold Ambedkarite literature on Ambedkar's birthday in front of the Indian Parliament in Delhi.

Valmiki mocks and rewrites the village pastoral that was long a staple of Indian literature in many languages, as well as a staple of the nationalist discourse of grassroots democracy. Valmiki portrays a village life where the members of his caste, Chuhras, lived outside the village, were forced to perform unpaid labor, and were denied basic requirements like access to public land and water, let alone education or camaraderie. Valmiki describes in painstaking detail the process of removing and skinning dead animals, curing the hide, and taking it to the hide market, which is permeated with the stench of raw hides and fresh bones. We read about the cleaning of stinking straw beds in the cattle sheds of higher-caste villagers. He describes the tasks involved in reaping and harvesting in terms of intense physical labor under a scorching sun and the needle pricks of the sheaves of grain. Valmiki shows that he performed most of these tasks under duress and was often paid nothing. The most painful of such episodes occurs when Fauza yanks Valmiki away from his books and drags him to his field to sow sugarcane just a day before Valmiki's math exam. Such a portrayal of village life is very unlike the lyric mode of Hindi nature poetry where the sickle-wielding, singing farmworker is just an accessory of the picturesque landscape.

Valmiki does not trust that his upper-caste readers will understand his point of view or believe the veracity of his experience. He preempts such responses by addressing them in his preface: "To those who say that these things do not to happen here, to those who want to claim a superior status for Indian civilization, I say that only those who have suffered this anguish know its sting." Every time Valmiki describes a violent encounter with the oppressor, he inserts the challenging and dissenting voices that constantly deny his testimony. By so doing, he provides readers with not only his experience as a victim but an inkling of how some people flatly deny such experiences ever occurred. His voice acquires a bitterly ironic tone when he addresses those who deny these experiences. In fact, one distinctive aspect of *Joothan*, which marks it as a Dalit text, is its interrogative discourse. The text is full of questions that demand an answer: "Why didn't an epic poet ever write a word about our lives?""Why is it a crime to ask to be paid for one's labor?" "Why are Hindus so cruel, so heartless against Dalits?" Such interrogatory rhetoric, which brings out the contradictions in the dominant society's ideology and behavior, reminds one of Ambedkar's fiery writing and speeches, which are peppered with witty, pungent, and harsh questions: "I asked them [our Hindu friends], 'You take the milk from the cows and buffaloes and when they are dead you expect us to remove the dead bodies. Why? If you carry the dead bodies of your mothers to cremate, why do you not carry the dead bodies of your "mother-cows" yourself?'" (Ambedkar 1969:143).

Valmiki, like many other Dalit writers, demands the status of truth for his writing, taking issue with those who find Dalit literature lacking in imagination. Valmiki dismisses imagination as make-believe, insisting that he writes about the "suffered real." Valmiki's critical writing repeatedly stresses the authentic portrayal of society as a Dalit literary value. One aspect of such an insistence on truth is Valmiki's use of real names in *Joothan*.

Valmiki's insistence that all people and events in *Joothan* are true poses a considerable challenge to postmodernist critics who propose that autobiography's truth is "constructed," that the autobiographic narrator shapes a presentable self by reprocessing his or her memories in order to fit the present. Dalit autobiography *claims* the status of truth, of testimony. Naming people and places by their real names is one strategy through which Valmiki establishes the status of *Joothan* as testimony. The concrete materiality of his village and the cities that he later inhabits, and the rendering of historical Dalit protests that he participated in or wrote about in the newspapers at a personal cost, give *Joothan* the status of documented Dalit history.

The timbre of his voice is exhortatory. It demands answers and points out contradictions. While the text has many moments of deep sadness and pathos, its predominant mood is irony. The narrative comments are inevitably in an ironic voice, pouring sarcasm on the cherished cultural ideals and myths of high-caste friends. Valmiki makes fun of their well-meaning advice to him to write about universals rather than about the "narrow circle" of particularism. He relentlessly exposes the double standards of friends who are greatly interested in literature and theater yet practice untouchability in subtle ways, such as having a different set of teacups for their untouchable visitors.

Indeed, *Joothan* demands a radical shift from the upper-caste and upper-class reader by insisting that such readers not forget their caste or class privilege. Unlike canonical Hindi or English writing, where the reader's, or the writer's, caste and class are often considered irrelevant, *Joothan*'s dual approach problematizes the reader's caste and class. While Valmiki directs his irony, satire, harangue, and anger at non-Dalit readers, he sees Dalit readers as fellow sufferers. Valmiki claims in his preface that his Dalit readers' letters enabled him to continue to expand his narrative after a fifteen-page autobiographical piece was published in a Dalit collection aptly titled *Harijan se Dalit* (From Harijan to Dalit).

While the indictment of an unjust social system and its benefactors is one thrust of the text, its other important preoccupation is a substantive examination of Dalit lives. *Joothan* combines representations of struggles with the external enemy and the enemy within: the internalization by Dalit people of upper-caste brahminic values, the superstitions of Dalit villagers, the patriarchal oppression of Dalit women by their men, the attempts by Dalits who have attained a middle-class economic status to "pass" as high caste and the attendant denial of their roots, their inferiority complex, which makes them criticize the practice of rural Dalits of rearing pigs—all these aspects of Dalit struggle are an equally important aspect of *Joothan*. This self-critique has earned him brickbats from many Dalits who find the frank portrayal of Dalit society to be humiliating. For them, it is tantamount to washing dirty linen in public. Valmiki accuses these Dalits of succumbing to brahminism. His frank critique of his own family members who hide their caste and therefore deny their relationship to Valmiki in public must have been painful to the people involved, particularly because he named them.

Joothan, then, is a multivalent, polyvocal text, healing the fractured self through narrating, contributing to the archive of Dalit history, opening a dialogue with the silencing oppressors, and providing solace as well as frank criticism to his own people. Its overall effect is truly paradoxical, for Valmiki's becoming a speaking subject shows that Indian democracy has opened some escape hatches through which a critical mass of articulate, educated Dalits has emerged. On the other hand, the harsh realities that he portrays so powerfully underscore the failure to fully meet the promises made in the Constitution of independent India. *Joothan* stridently asks for the promissory note, joining a chorus of Dalit voices that are demanding their rightful place under the sun. A manifesto for revolutionary transformation of society and human consciousness, *Joothan* confronts its readers with difficult questions about their own humanity and invites them to join the universal project of human liberation.

I do hope that this English translation of *Joothan* conveys the timbre of Valmiki's voice: its honesty, its anger, its mockery, and its sadness. No translation is a replica of the original text, and every translation necessarily entails a loss. My translation of *Joothan* is no exception. At times the English version may sound awkward, but I have chosen awkwardness over falsification or softening. For example, the Hindi term *jatak*, as used by the village upper castes, does not translate as *child* or *children* because these English words have positive connotations. I have therefore used *progeny* to convey the coldness and contempt in caste-inflected interactions.

It has, of course, been impossible to convey the different registers of Valmiki's Hindi. The speech and conversations of his family and villagers are in local dialect but with distinct variations, the linguistic equivalent of the social distance between them. The differences between the adult narrator's literary Hindi and the dialect attributed to his childhood self poignantly mark the emotional and physical distance that Valmiki has traveled from illiteracy to literacy, from the village to the city.

All cross-cultural communication involves a loss in meaning. Valmiki constantly worries whether *savarna* Hindus who have not experienced the hardships of untouchability will understand him. Dalit literary theory cautions us against notions of mastery of Dalit texts, reminding us that the Dalits' life worlds have been shaped differently because they had to make do with other people's garbage and *joothan*. Limbale proposes that what the readers and critics need more than anything else when reading Dalit writing is empathy. Rejecting the traditional apparatus for evaluating and understanding texts because it is infected with caste- and class-based values, Limbale suggests that we measure the success of a Dalit text by how powerfully it affects the reader's consciousness. If this translated version of *Joothan* manages to engage readers by appealing to their consciousness and arousing their empathy, it will have done its job.

DELHI AND TORONTO
AUGUST 2002

REFERENCES

Ambedkar, B. R. 1969. *Thus Spoke Ambedkar: Selected Speeches*. Vol. 2. Edited by Bhagwan Das. Jullundur, India: Bheem Patrika Publications.

———. [1979] 1989a. "Annihilation of Caste with a Reply to Mahatma Gandhi" [1936, 1944]. In *Dr. Babasaheb Ambedkar: Writings and Speeches*. Vol. 1. Compiled by Vasant Moon. Bombay: Education Department, Government of Maharashtra.

———. 1989b. *Dr. Babasaheb Ambedkar: Writings and Speeches*. Vol. 5. Edited by Vasant Moon. Bombay: Education Department, Government of Maharashtra.

———. 1990. *The Untouchables: Who Were They and Why They Became Untouchables?* (1948). In *Dr. Babasaheb Ambedkar: Writings and Speeches*. Vol. 7. Edited by Vasant Moon. Bombay: Education Department, Government of Maharashtra.

Dangle, Arjun. 1992. "Dalit Literature, Past, Present, and Future." In Arjun Dangle, ed., *Poisoned Bread: Translations from Modern Marathi Dalit Literature*, pp. 234–36. Translated by Avinash S. Pandit and Daya Agarwal. Bombay: Orient Longman.

Das, Bhagwan. n.d. "Editorial Note on the History of the Conversion Movement Launched by Dr. Ambedkar on 13 October 1935 at Yeola, District Nasik, Bombay." In *Thus Spoke Ambedkar: Selected Speeches*. Vol. 4. Edited by Bhagwan Das. Bangalore, India: Ambedkar Sahitya Prakashan.

———. 1995. "Socio-Economic Problems of Dalits." In *Dalit Solidarity*. Edited by Bhagwan Das and James Massey. Delhi: Indian Society for the Promoting Christian Knowledge.

Ilaiah, Kancha. 1996. *Why I Am Not a Hindu: A Sudra Critique of Hindutva Philosophy, Culture, and Political Economy*. Calcutta: Samya.

Kosambi, Damodar Dharmanand. [1975] 1995. *An Introduction to the Study of Indian History*. Bombay: Popular Prakashan.

Lal, A. C. 1995. "Opening Address: Dalit Solidarity Conference, Nagpur, 1992." In *Dalit Solidarity*. Edited by Bhagwan Das and James Massey. Delhi: Indian Society for the Promoting Christian Knowledge.

Limbale, Sharankumar. 2004. *Towards an Aesthetic of Dalit Literature: History, Controversies, and Considerations*. Translated by Alok Mukherjee. Hyderabad, India: Orient Longman.

Mukherjee, Prabhati. 1988. *Beyond the Four Varnas: The Untouchables in India*. Shimla, India: Indian Institute of Advanced Study.

Omvedt, Gail. 1994. *Dalits and the Democratic Revolution: Dr. Ambedkar and the Dalit Movement in Colonial India*. Delhi: Sage.

———. 1996. *Dalit Visions: The Anti-Caste Movement and the Construction of an Indian Identity*. Delhi: Orient Longman.

Valmiki, Omprakash. 2001. *Dalit Sahitya ka Saundaryashastra*. Delhi: Radhakrishna.

Wankhade, M. N. 1992. "Friends, the Day of Irresponsible Writing Is Over." In Arjun Dangle, ed., *Poisoned Bread: Translations from Modern Marathi Dalit Literature*, pp. 314–23. Translated by Maxine Berntsen. Bombay: Orient Longman.

JOOTHAN

OUR HOUSE WAS NEXT TO Chandrabhan Taga's cattle shed. Families of Muslim weavers lived on the other side of it. Right in front of the cattle shed was a little pond that had created a sort of partition between the Chuhras' dwellings and the village. The pond was called Dabbowali, and it is hard to say how it got that name. Perhaps because its shape was that of a big pit. On one side of the pit were the high walls of the brick homes of the Tagas. At a right angle to these were the clay walls of the two or three homes of the Jhinwars, another untouchable caste. After these were more homes of the Tagas.

The homes of the Chuhras were on the edges of the pond. All the women of the village, young girls, older women, even the newly married brides, would sit in the open space behind these homes at the edges of the pond to take a shit. Not just under the cover of darkness but even in daylight. The purdah-observing Tyagi women, their faces covered with their saris, shawls around their shoulders, found relief in this open-air latrine.[1] They sat on Dabbowali's shores without worrying about decency, exposing their private parts. All the quarrels of the village would be discussed in the style of a round-table conference at the same spot. The muck was strewn everywhere. The stench was so overpowering that one would choke within a minute. The pigs wandering in narrow lanes, naked children, dogs, daily fights—this was the environment of my childhood. If the people who call the caste sys-

---

1. Taga is the abbreviation of the surname Tyagi.

tem an ideal social arrangement had to live in this environment for a day or two, they would change their mind.

Our family lived in this Chuhra *basti*.[2] Five sons, one daughter, and our uncles—two *chachas*, one *tau*, and his family.[3] *Chachas* and *tau* lived separately. Everyone in the family did some work or other. Even then we didn't manage to get two decent meals a day. We did all sorts of work for the Tagas, including cleaning their homes, agricultural work, and general labor. We would often have to work without pay. Nobody dared to refuse this unpaid work for which we got neither money nor grain. Instead, we got sworn at and abused. They did not call us by our names. If a person was elderly, then he would be called "Oe, Chuhre." If the person was younger than we were or of the same age, then he would be addressed as "Abey, Chuhre."[4]

Untouchability was so rampant that while it was considered all right to touch dogs and cats or cows and buffaloes, if one [a higher-caste person] happened to touch a Chuhra, one got contaminated or polluted. The Chuhras were not seen as human. They were simply things for use. Their utility lasted until the work was done. Use them and then throw them away.

A Christian used to visit our neighborhood. His name was Sewak Ram Masihi. He would sit with the children of the Chuhras around him. He used to teach us reading and writing. The government schools did not allow us to enroll. My family sent only me to Sewak Ram Masihi. My brothers were all working. There was no question of sending our sister to school. I learned my alphabet in Master Sewak Ram Masihi's open-air school, a school without mats or rooms. One day Sewak Ram Masihi and my father had an argument. My father took me to the Basic Primary School. There my father begged Master Har Phool

---

2. *Basti* refers to settlement. In the villages the huts would be built of mud, and usually people of the same caste would live side by side.

3. See these and other kinship terms listed in the glossary.

4. These are slighting, pejorative ways of addressing someone: "You, Chuhre."

Singh: "Masterji, I will be forever in your debt if you teach this child of mine a letter or two."[5]

Master Har Phool Singh asked us to return the next day. My father went. He kept going for several days. Finally, one day I was admitted to the school. The country had become independent eight years earlier. Gandhiji's uplifting of the untouchables was having ramifications everywhere. Although the doors of the government schools had begun to open for untouchables, the mentality of the ordinary people had not changed much. I had to sit away from the others in the class, and even that wasn't enough. I was not allowed to sit on a chair or a bench. I had to sit on the bare floor; I was not allowed even to sit on the mat. Sometimes I would have to sit way behind everybody, right near the door. From there, the letters on the board seemed faded.

The children of the Tyagis would tease me by calling me "Chuhre ka."[6] Sometimes they would beat me for no reason. This was an absurd, tormented life that made me introverted and irritable. If I got thirsty in school, then I had to stand near the hand pump.[7] The boys would beat me in any case, but the teachers also punished me. They tried all sorts of strategies so that I would run away from the school and take up the kind of work for which I was born. According to these perpetrators, my attempts to get schooling were not justifiable.

Ram Singh and Sukkhan Singh were also in my class. Ram Singh was of the Chamar caste and Sukkhan Singh was a Jhinwar, both untouchables like me. Ram Singh's father and mother

5. In general, few adults are called simply by their first names. In northern India, where this autobiography is set, speakers always add the honorific *ji* as a courtesy suffix, because simply calling someone by a name is seen as presumptuous and rude; some people also believe that a name is something powerful, not to be taken lightly. In this context, to call to a person with "Abey, Chuhre" is extremely derogatory.

6. This is a pejorative that means, "You, offspring of the Chuhras." *Ka* is the possessive case here meaning Chuhr'es offspring; *ke* is the vocative case of addressive: "Hey, you Chuhra."

7. He had to stand near the pump and wait for someone from another caste who could touch the pump to notice and give him some water. If an untouchable touched the hand pump, it would need "purification" before the other castes could use it.

worked as agricultural laborers. Sukkhan Singh's father was a peon in the Inter College [a junior high school]. The three of us studied together, grew up together, experienced the sweet and sour moments of childhood together. All three of us were very good in our studies, but our extremely lower-caste background dogged us at every step.

Barla Village also had some Muslim Tyagis who were called Tagas as well. The behavior of these Muslim Tagas was just like that of the Hindu Tagas. If we ever went out wearing neat and clean clothes, we had to hear their taunts that pierced deep inside, like poisoned arrows. If we went to school in neat and clean clothes, our classmates said, "Abey, Chuhre ka, he has come dressed in new clothes." If we went wearing old and shabby clothes, then they said, "Abey, Chuhre ke, get away from me, you stink."

This was our no-win situation. We were humiliated whichever way we dressed.

I reached fourth class.[8] Kaliram had replaced the headmaster, Bishambar Singh. Along with him had come another new teacher. After the arrival of these two, the three of us fell on terrible times. They would thrash us at the slightest excuse. Ram Singh would escape once in a while, but Sukkhan Singh and I got beaten almost daily. I was very weak and skinny in those days.

Sukkhan Singh developed a boil on his belly, just below his ribs. While in class, he used to keep his shirt folded up to keep the boil uncovered. This way the shirt could be kept clear of the puss, and he thought that if the teacher could see the boil, he would be decent and not hit him. One day the teacher's fist hit the boil while he was thrashing Sukkhan Singh. Sukkhan screamed with pain. The boil had burst. Seeing him flailing with pain, I too began to cry. While we cried, the teacher was showering abuse on us non-stop. If I repeated his abusive words here, they would smear the nobility of Hindi. I say that, because many big-name Hindi writers wrinkled their noses and eyebrows when I had a character

---

8. Students in the fourth class are around ten years old.

swear in my short story "Bail ki Khal" (The Ox Hide). Coincidentally, the character who swore was a Brahmin, that is, the knower of Brahma, of God. Was it possible? Would a Brahmin swear?

The ideal image of the teachers that I saw in my childhood has remained indelibly imprinted on my memory. Whenever someone starts talking about a great guru, I remember all those teachers who used to swear about mothers and sisters. They used to fondle good-looking boys and invite them to their homes and sexually abuse them.

One day the headmaster, Kaliram, called me to his room and asked: "Abey, what is your name?"

"Omprakash," I answered slowly and fearfully. Children used to feel scared just encountering the headmaster. The entire school was terrified of him.

"Chuhre ka?" the headmaster threw his second question at me.

"Ji."

"All right. See that teak tree there? Go. Climb that tree. Break some twigs and make a broom. And sweep the whole school clean as a mirror. It is, after all, your family occupation.

"Go—get to it."

Obeying the headmaster's orders, I cleaned all the rooms and the verandas. Just as I was about to finish, he came to me and said, "After you have swept the rooms, go and sweep the playground."

The playground was much larger than my small physique could handle, and in cleaning it my back began to ache. My face was covered with dust. I had dust inside my mouth. The other children in my class were studying and I was sweeping. The headmaster was sitting in his room and watching me. I was not even allowed to get a drink of water. I swept the whole day. I had never done so much work, being the pampered one among my brothers.

The second day, as soon as I reached school, the headmaster again put me to sweeping the school. I swept the whole day. I was consoling myself that I would go back to class the next day.

The third day I went to the class and sat down quietly. After a few minutes the headmaster's loud thundering was heard: "Abey, Chuhre ke, motherfucker, where are you hiding your mother?"

I began to shake uncontrollably. A Tyagi boy shouted, "Master Sahib, there he is, sitting in the corner."

The headmaster pounced on my neck. The pressure of his fingers was increasing. As a wolf grabs a lamb by the neck, he dragged me out of the class and threw me on the ground. He screamed: "Go sweep the whole playground—otherwise I will shove chilis up your ass and throw you out of the school."

Frightened, I picked up the three-day-old broom. Just like me, it was shedding its dried up leaves. All that remained were the thin sticks. Tears were falling from my eyes. I started to sweep the compound while my tears fell. From the doors and windows of the schoolrooms, the teachers and the boys saw this spectacle. Each pore of my body was submerged in an abyss of anguish.

Just then my father passed by the school. He stopped abruptly when he saw me sweeping the school compound. He called me: "Munshiji, what are you doing?" Munshiji was the pet name my father had given me. When I saw him, I burst out sobbing. He entered the school compound and came toward me. Seeing me crying, he asked, "Munshiji, why are you crying? Tell me, what has happened?"

I was hiccuping by now. In between my hiccups I told the whole story to my father: that the teachers had been making me sweep for the last three days, that they did not let me enter the classroom at all.

Pitaji snatched the broom from my hand and threw it away. His eyes were blazing. Pitaji, who was always taut as a bowstring in front of others, was so angry that his dense moustache was fluttering. He began to scream, "Who is that teacher, that progeny of Dronacharya, who forces my son to sweep?"

Pitaji's voice had echoed through the whole school. All the teachers, along with the headmaster, came out. Kaliram, the headmaster, threatened my father and called him names. But his threats had no effect on Pitaji. I have never forgotten the courage and the fortitude with which my father confronted the headmaster that day. Pitaji had all sorts of weaknesses, but the decisive turn that he gave my future that day has had a great influence on my personality.

The headmaster had roared, "Take him away from here. The Chuhra wants him educated. Go, go—otherwise I will have your bones broken."

Pitaji took my hand and started walking toward our home. As he walked away, he said, loud enough for the headmaster to hear, "You are a teacher. So I am leaving now. But remember this much, Master: This Chuhre ka will study right here, in this school. And not just him, there will be more coming after him."

Pitaji had faith that the Tyagis of the village would chastise Master Kaliram for his behavior. But what happened was the exact opposite. On whatever door we knocked, the answer was, "What is the point of sending him to school?"

Or, "When has a crow become a swan?"

Or, "You illiterate boorish people, what do you know? Knowledge is not gained like this."

"Hey, if he asked a Chuhra's progeny to sweep, what is the big deal in that?"

Or, "He only got him to sweep; did not ask for his thumb in the *gurudakshina* like Dronacharya."

And so forth.

Pitaji came back, tired and dejected. He sat up all night without food or drink. God knows how deep an anguish Pitaji went through. As soon as the morning broke, he took me along and went to the house of the *pradhan*, or village chief, Sagwa Singh Tyagi.

As soon as the *pradhan* saw Pitaji, he said, "Abey, Chotan? . . . What is the matter? You have come so early in the morning."

"Chowdhuri Sahib, you say that the government has opened the doors of the schools for the children of Chuhras and Chamars. And that headmaster makes this child of mine to come out of the class and sweep all day instead of teaching him. If he has to sweep the school all day, then you tell me: When is he going to study?"

Pitaji was supplicating the *pradhan*. He had tears in his eyes. I was standing near him and looking at him.

The *pradhan* called me near him and asked, "Which class are you in?"

"Ji, the fourth."

"You are in my Mahendra's class?"

"Ji."

Pradhanji said to Pitaji, "Don't worry. Send him to school tomorrow."

The next day I went to school with fear stalking my heart. I sat in the class in trepidation. Every second I worried that the headmaster was coming . . . Now he comes . . . At the slightest sound my heart pounded. After a few days things calmed down. But my heart trembled the moment I saw Headmaster Kaliram. It seemed as though it wasn't a teacher who was coming toward me but a snorting wild boar with his snout up in the air.

———

At harvest time all the people in our neighborhood would have to go to the field of the Tagas to reap the crop. Cutting the sheaves of wheat in the midday sun is a very hard and painful task. The sun pours on your head. Fiery-hot ground is beneath you. The roots of the cropped wheat plants pricked our feet like spikes. The roots of mustard and *chana* dal hurt even more.[9] The harvesting of these lentils presents an extra difficulty. The leaves are sour and stick all over the body. Even bathing does not get rid of them completely. Most of the reapers were from the untouchable castes of the Chuhras or Chamars. They had clothes on their bodies in name only. There was no question of shoes on their feet. Their bare feet were badly injured by the time the crop was brought in.

The harvesting would often lead to arguments in the fields. Most Tagas were miserly about paying wages. The reapers were

———

9. Yellow lentils, one of the many varieties of dal eaten in India.

helpless. Whatever they got, they took after some protest. After coming back home, they would fret, cursing the Tagas. But their protests died when confronted with hunger. Every year there would be a meeting in the neighborhood at harvest time. People swore to demand one sheaf out of sixteen as wages. But all the resolutions passed at the meetings evaporated in thin air the moment harvesting began. For wages they got one sheaf for cutting twenty-one sheaves. One sheaf was less than a kilo of grain. Even the heaviest sheaf did not yield a kilo of wheat. That is, a day's wage wasn't worth even a kilo of wheat. After the harvesting the grain had to be loaded on bullock or buffalo carts and unloaded. Neither money nor grain was given for that work. Sooner or later all of us had to drive the bullocks onto the threshing floor, again without payment. In those days we didn't have threshers for cleaning up the wheat. The bullocks would be taken round and round to break down the sheaves into straw. Then the grain would be separated from the chaff by blowing it in a winnow. It was very long and tiring work, work performed mostly by Chamars or Chuhras.

Along with these field labors, my mother also cleaned the *baithaks*, the outer room or space that men used as their space for chatting or meeting, and the cattle sheds of eight or ten Tagas, both Hindus and Muslims.[10] My sister, elder *bhabhi*—sister-in-law—and my two brothers, Jasbir and Janesar, helped my mother in this work. My oldest brother, Sukhbir, worked for the Tagas like a permanent servant.

Every Taga would have ten to fifteen animals in his cowshed. We would have to pick up their dung and bring it to the place where *uplas*, or cow-dung cakes, were made. We would take five to six baskets of dung from every cowshed. During the winter months it was a very painful job. The cows, buffaloes, and bullocks

---

10. The *baithak* was out of bounds to women.

would be tethered in long hallways. The floor would be covered
with the dry leaves of cane or straw. The dung and the urine of the
animals would spread all over the floor overnight. We would
change the matting after ten or fifteen days. Or sometimes we
would add a layer of dry leaves on top of the soiled one. To search
for dung in the stinking cowsheds was extremely unpleasant. The
stink made one feel faint.

To compensate us for all this work, we got five seers of grain
per two animals; that is, about 2.5 kilos of grain. Each Taga household with ten animals gave twenty-five seers of grain a year—
about twelve to fifteen kilos; we got a leftover roti at noon every
day that was specially made by mixing the flour with husk because
it was for the Chuhras. Sometimes the *joothan*, the half-eaten
scraps, would also be put in the basket with the rotis for us.

During a wedding, when the guests and the *baratis*, those who
had accompanied the bridegroom as members of his party, were
eating their meals, the Chuhras would sit outside with huge baskets. After the bridegroom's party had eaten, the dirty *pattals*, or
leaf plates, were put in the Chuhras' baskets, which they took
home, to save the *joothan* that was sticking to them. The little remnants of *pooris*, puffed bread; bits of sweetmeats; and a little bit of
vegetable were enough to make them happy. They ate the *joothan*
with a lot of relish. They denounced as gluttons the bridegroom's
guests who didn't leave enough scraps on their leaf plates. Poor
things, they had never enjoyed a wedding feast. So they had licked
it all up. During the marriage season our elders narrated, in
thrilled voices, stories of the bridegroom's party that had left several months of *joothan*.

We dried in the sun the pieces of *pooris* that we collected from
the leaf plates. We would spread a cloth on a *charpai*, a rope-string
cot, to dry them. Often, I would be placed on guard duty because
the drying *pooris* attracted crows, hens, and dogs. Even a moment's
lapse and the *pooris* would vanish. Hence one would have to sit
near the cot with a stick in hand.

These dried-up *pooris* were useful during the hard days of the rainy season. We would soak them in water and then boil them. The boiled *pooris* were delicious with finely ground red chili pepper and salt. Sometimes we mixed them with *gur* to make a gruel and ate this dish with great delight.[11]

When I think about all those things today, thorns begin to prick my heart. What sort of a life was that? After working hard day and night, the price of our sweat was just *joothan*. And yet no one had any grudges. Or shame. Or repentance.

When I was a young boy, I used to go with my parents to help them out. Looking at the food of the Tagas, I would wonder why we never got to eat food like that. When I think of those days today, I feel nauseated.

This past year Sukhdev Singh Tyagi's grandson, Surendra, visited my house in connection with some interview. He had obtained my address in the village. He stayed the night with us. My wife fed him a nice meal, and while eating, he said, "Bhabhiji, you make such delicious food. No one in our family can cook so well."[12] His compliment made my wife happy, but I was deeply disturbed for quite some time. The incidents of childhood began knocking at my memory's door again.

Surendra had not even been born then. His aunt, that is, Sukhdev Singh Tyagi's daughter, was getting married. My mother used to clean their place. For ten to twelve days before the wedding my parents were doing all sorts of work at Sukhdev Singh Tyagi's home. A daughter's wedding meant that the prestige of the whole village was at stake. Everything had to be perfect. My father went from village to village to collect rope-string cots for the guests.

The bridegroom's party was eating. My mother was sitting outside the door with her basket. I and my sister Maya, who was younger than I, sat close to my mother in the hope that we too

---

11. *Gur* means molasses, which is less expensive than sugar.

12. Another sign of courtesy, and of intimacy or friendship, is to turn nonkin into kin by addressing a person by using a kinship term like *bhabhi* (sister-in-law). Here, Sukhdev Singh Tyagi, who is not related to the author or his wife, turns her into honorary kin by addressing her as Bhabhiji.

would get a share of the sweets and the gourmet dishes that we could smell cooking inside.

When all the people had left after the feast, my mother said to Sukhdev Singh Tyagi, as he was crossing the courtyard to come to the front door: "Chowdhuriji, all of your guests have eaten and gone. . . . Please put something on a leaf plate for my children. They too have waited for this day."

Sukhdev Singh pointed at the basket full of dirty leaf plates and said, "You are taking a basketful of *joothan*. And on top of that you want food for your children? Don't forget your place, Chuhri.[13] Pick up your basket and get going."

Those words of Sukhdev Singh Tyagi's penetrated my breast like a knife. They continue to singe me to this day.

That night the mother goddess Durga entered my mother's eyes. It was the first time that I saw my mother get so angry. She emptied the basket right there. She said to Sukhdev Singh, "Pick it up and put it inside your house. Feed it to the bridegroom's guests tomorrow morning." She gathered me and my sister and left like an arrow. Sukhdev Singh had pounced on her to hit her, but my mother had confronted him like a lioness. Without being afraid.

After that day Ma never went back to his door. And after this incident she also stopped taking their *joothan*.

The same Sukhdev Singh came to my house one day. My wife welcomed him with open arms, treating him with the respect due a village elder. He *did* eat at our house. But after he left, my nephew Sanjaya Khairwal, who was studying for his bachelor of science degree, said to me, "Chachaji, he ate only at your own house; at our place, he did not even drink water."

My oldest brother, Sukhbir, was a year-round servant at Suchet Taga's. I was in fifth class then. He would have been around twenty-five or

---

13. *Churhi* is a derogatory way of addressing a woman of the Chuhra caste.

twenty-six years of age. He was very dark complexioned, tall, and muscular. One day a wild boar came inside the village. He had injured a lot of people with his sharp horns. He went into the cowsheds of the Tagas and injured the oxen, buffaloes, and cows. All the people climbed on the rooftops to watch this spectacle. No Taga showed the courage to catch the wild boar and throw him out of the village.

Sukhbir was returning from Suchet's field at the time. When he asked the screaming and shouting Tagas on the rooftops what had happened, they told him about the boar. Sukhbir drove that boar out of the village with just a stick. His confidence and strength impressed the whole village. They discussed his feat for a long time after that.

One day when he returned from work, his body was hot with fever. He was in bed for a week. He died for lack of proper medication or treatment. It was as though lightning had struck our family. Everything had scattered. Pitaji was totally broken by this tragedy. Mother was so overwhelmed by Sukhbir's death that she would faint at short intervals. Bhabhi, our sister-in-law, became a widow at a young age. Our family's situation, which had been improving because of my brother, now took a turn for the worse. I remember that since our brother began to work, no younger brothers, sister, or sister-in-law had worked in a Taga's house. I never had to sweep anybody's house.

After my brother's death my father and my uncle joined a road construction crew. They would take on whatever job they were offered.

In our community widow remarriage was an accepted practice. Unlike the Hindu tradition, we did not see widow marriage negatively. In the presence of relatives and village elders, the father of my widowed sister-in-law betrothed her to Jasbir, the brother who was the next in line to Sukhbir. Everyone in our community accepted this arrangement. At that time Sukhbir's son, Narendra, was about one-and-a-half years old, and his widow was pregnant. Devendra was born six or seven months after my brother's death.

After Sukhbir's death the entire burden of the family had fall-
en on Jasbir's shoulders. Whatever we could earn in the village was
not enough to make ends meet. The financial condition of the
family was precarious. One day Jasbir left for Adampur to work
for a construction company, Tirath Ram and Company. In those
days an airport was being built in Adampur, which is in Punjab,
for the Indian air force. After some time that company moved to
Bagdogra, Bengal, to build the airport there. Jasbir's letter came
many months after he went to Bagdogra.

Ma threw a tantrum when she heard that he was in Bengal.
Mother's idea of Bengal was based on folk myths about black
magic and casting of spells, about women who transformed a man
into a ram with their magic and tied him up in their courtyard.
Her Bengal was not the Bengal of Rabindranath Tagore or the rev-
olutionaries.[14] After we got the letter, Ma cried day and night,
"One son has left the world and the other is in a foreign land." A
pall fell on the house. Our sister-in-law was ill. There was not
enough food for us all. We ate whatever we could scramble together. No one laughed; no one talked.

Our sister-in-law would sit wordlessly, her head on her knees.
All of us seemed to have become locked in our shells.

I had passed class five. I had to gain admission to the sixth.
The village was the home of Tyagi Inter College, Barla, which has
since changed its name to Barla Inter College, Barla. I would not
be able to gain admission, given the circumstances that the family
found itself in. How could one think of studies when one didn't
even have food?

My heart would become heavy when I saw my schoolmates
passing by with books in their hands. Janesar was one of my older
brothers [the brother closest to the author in age]. We would both
leave home early in the morning. We would go around the fields,
collecting wild grass for our buffalo. A few days before his death,

14. Rabindranath Tagore (1861–1941), the Bengali author and painter, won the Nobel
Prize for Literature in 1913.

Sukhbir had acquired the buffalo in barter from Suchet Taga. We hoped to make some money when she calved. Attending to the buffalo kept me and Janesar busy. I also had the responsibility of grazing the pigs in the afternoon. Pigs were an important part of our lives. In sickness or in health, in life or in death, in wedding ceremonies—pigs played an important role in all of them. Even our religious ceremonies were incomplete without the pigs. The pigs rooting in the compound were not symbols of dirt to us but of prosperity, and so they are today. Yes, the educated among us, who are still a minute percentage, have abandoned these conventions. It is not because of a reformist perspective but because of their inferiority complex that they have done so. The educated ones suffer more from this inferiority complex, which is caused by social pressures.

One day I was coming home after grazing the pigs. On the way home I met Sukkhan Singh, who stopped me and asked, "Why have you stopped coming to school? Aren't you going to study further?" I shook my head in refusal. He kept talking a long time about the new atmosphere of the school. Now it had desks and chairs, whereas before we used to sit on mats. The teachers also did not beat the students as much. And there was a separate teacher for each subject.

I returned home with a sad heart. Something was bubbling inside me. I had lost all hope because I could not go to school. The majestic building of the Inter College was constantly before my eyes. As soon as I returned home, I said to my mother, "Ma, I want to go to school." There were tears in my eyes. Seeing my tears, my mother also started to cry. When Ma cried, she would recount her complaints and grudges in a loud voice that brought forth all the neighborhood women, who would surround her. The harder they tried to console Ma, the harder Ma wept.

Our sister-in-law was crying too, sitting all by herself. My brother's death had caused a wedge between her and the rest of the family. Bhabhi had a silver anklet that she kept with great care with her wedding outfits.

Ma was crying as loudly as ever. Bhabhi opened her tin box, took out the anklet, and put it in Ma's hand.

"Sell it and get Lallaji admitted." All the women were overwhelmed by her affectionate gesture. I embraced Bhabhi and cried. At that moment I missed my brother deeply. The memory of that day still continues to empower me.

Pitaji had tried hard to dissuade his daughter-in-law. "No, Bahu . . . don't sell it. I will arrange somehow to send him to school. Don't you worry . . . You have just the one ornament . . . How can we sell that too? . . . Go on, keep it."

But Bhabhi wouldn't listen to him and insisted on putting it in Ma's hand.

Vaidya Satyanarayana Sharma had a pawnshop, and he would buy gold and silver ornaments and act as a moneylender in addition to his regular job as the village priest. Ma pawned the anklet with him, and thus was I admitted to class six.

Ram Singh and Sukkhan Singh were in a different section. My roll number was right at the end, and therefore I sat in the last row. Shravankumar Sharma [a Brahmin] sat in the next seat. Although we had been studying together since class one, now we became really close because of our sitting together. Shravankumar was handsome and attractive. Delicate like a girl. Caste never came between us. This was a unique experience for me. Ram Singh and Sukkhan Singh were also my classmates, but Sukkhan Singh never came to my house. I would often go to his house. We sat together, studied together. Later on we also developed relationships at the family level. Today his older son, Rajneesh, treats me and my wife with a great deal of respect.

Perhaps Sukkhan Singh was a little remote, unlike Shravankumar. Then we became friends with a third person. His name was Chandrapal Varma, and he came from the village of Mandla. He was a Gujjar by caste.[15] He used to bother

15. Gujjar is a middle caste found in northern and central India and is considered to be above the Tyagis.

Shravankumar a lot. Sometimes he would pinch his cheeks and sometimes he would push him. Sometimes he would hide his books. These were daily occurrences.

One day, as we were coming out of the classroom, Chandrapal Varma gripped Shravankumar tightly and bit him on his cheek. The whole class saw him do it, but no one said a word. Everyone was laughing loudly. Shravankumar began to cry. Chandrapal Varma was also laughing. I don't know what happened to me at that moment, but I grabbed Chandrapal's neck and pushed him down, even though he was twice my height and weight. Chandrapal kept squirming to free his neck, but I did not let go of him. Chandrapal did not get angry with me but kept laughing. Later he also begged forgiveness from Shravankumar.

The three of us became good friends after this incident. Our friendship was so deep that we felt incomplete without each other. After school Shravankumar and I did not take the main road home. We walked home through the fields and the footpaths. This became a regular routine of ours. My friendship with Chandrapal made an immediate difference in my life. I was released from the taunts and the scoldings of the Tyagi boys. Now I did not have to stand waiting near the tap for a drink of water. They all lost their tongues when Chandrapal was around. He could hit anyone he wanted. Chandrapal aside, the Tyagi boys were afraid of the Gujjar boys.

I stood first in my section in the half-yearly exam. My results bolstered my self-confidence. I was made the class monitor after the examination, and my seat was moved from the back of the class to the front. The behavior of some teachers, however, was still unfriendly. They were indifferent and contemptuous of me.

I WAS KEPT OUT OF extracurricular activities. On such occasions I stood on the margins like a spectator. During the annual functions of the school, such as rehearsals for the play, I too wished for a role. But I always had to stand outside the door. The so-called descendants of the gods cannot understand the anguish of standing outside the door.

All the teachers were Tyagis, and among the students Tyagis were the majority too. No one could afford to say anything against them. During examinations we could not drink water from the glass when we were thirsty. To drink water we had to cup our hands. The peon [office boy] would pour water from way high up, lest our hands touch the glass.

The school had a library where books were gathering dust. There I first became acquainted with books. By the time I reached class eight, I had read Saratchandra, Premchand, and Rabindranath Tagore.[1] Saratchandra's characters had touched my child's heart very deeply. I had become somewhat of an introvert, and reading was my main passion.

I began to read novels and short stories to my mother by the faint light of the wick lamp. Who knows how often Saratchandra's characters have made a mother and son cry together? This was the

---

1. Students in class eight are around fourteen years old. Saratchandra Chattopadhyay (1876–1938) was an acclaimed Bengali novelist, short story writer, and essayist whose writings are considered canonical and are still immensely popular. They were translated into many Indian languages during his lifetime. Among his famous novels are *Srikanta*, *Charitraheen*, *Grihadaha*, and *Devdas*. He delineated female characters with great sympathy. Dhanpath Rai Srivastava (1880–1936) wrote under the pen name of Premchand; he is considered to be one of the most distinguished writers of modern Hindi and Urdu literature.

beginning of my literary sensibility. Starting from *Alha,* the *Ramayana,* and the *Mahabharata* to *Sur Sagar, Prem Sagar, Sukh Sagar,* Premchand's stories, *Kissa Tota Maina*—whatever I found, I, the son of an untouchable illiterate family, read to my mother.

In April 1993 I received an invitation from Rajendra Yadavji, editor of *Hans.* He had organized a program called "Katha Kathan" in the laborers' colonies of Delhi, and I was among those who got the chance to tell their stories there. The first event was at the Valmiki Temple at Mandir Marg. I experienced a strange emotion while telling my story. That day the memories of my mother became fresh all of a sudden. What better way to bridge the gap between literature and the public than an event such as Katha Kathan? The illiterate masses cannot read literature. Those who can read are unable to buy books. Katha Kathan provided an avenue for a meaningful dialogue between audience and writers.

As my studies advanced, I began to lose touch with my neighborhood friends who did not go to school. Satpal and Hiram Singh of the *basti* had started going to school. So only three boys out of thirty families in our *basti* went to school.

Ram Singh, Sukkham Singh, and I were together once again after class six.[2] Ram Singh was the brightest of us all. Ram Singh and I had joined the Scouts. The Scouts had to go to the city for a district-level meeting. The school issued us khaki shorts and shirts. The Scout leader, Rameshchand, had asked that the uniform be washed and ironed. Up to that point I had never worn an ironed piece of clothing. Whenever I saw the starched and freshly washed clothes of the Tyagi boys, I wished that I too could go to school in such clothes. At times I had to wear hand-me-downs from the Tyagis. The boys teased me when they saw those clothes. But even the hand-me-downs could not cover our helplessness.

I washed that khaki uniform with great care. The problem was how to iron it. A boy in my class was the son of a *dhobi,* or washerman. I asked him for help. He told me to come to his house in

---

2. Students in class six are around twelve years old.

the evening. I took the uniform to his house that evening. As soon as his father saw me, he screamed, "Abey, Chuhre ka, where do you think you are going?" His son was standing near him. I said, "I need to have the uniform ironed."

"We don't wash the clothes of the Chuhra-Chamars. Nor do we iron them. If we iron your clothes, then the Tagas won't get their clothes washed by us. We will lose our roti." He had answered me bluntly. His reply crushed me. I left without saying a word. My heart was heavy. I lost faith in God. One can somehow get past poverty and deprivation, but it is impossible to get past caste.

I had a teacher named Yogendra Tyagi who was from Kutubpur. He was a nice man and a good teacher. He taught history and English. I used to be impressed by the way he rattled off dates in history. I felt that he had a great knowledge of history. It was he who made me interested in history, an interest that I have retained to this day. He knew my father. Whenever he saw Pitaji, he would tell him, "Chotan, don't prevent your son from studying."

Despite all his good intentions, he used to cause me great distress in the classroom. Whenever I made a mistake, instead of thrashing me, he would grab my shirt and pull it toward him. All my concentration would then be focused on my shirt, as I feared that it would get ripped apart at any moment. Pulling me by the shirt, he would ask, "How many pieces of pork did you eat? You must have eaten at least half a pound."

Whenever Master Sahib said things like that, I would begin to cry. My eyes would fill up. The whole class used to laugh at Master Sahib's comments. The boys would torment me about them. "Abey, Chuhre ke, you eat pork." At such moments I would think of all the Tyagis who came in the darkness of the night to the Bhangi [untouchables, the Chuhras are a subcaste] basti to eat pork. I felt like calling out the names of all those people. Those who came to eat meat secretly at night observed untouchability in daylight in front of everybody.

One of these was Teja Taga. Many people borrowed money from him. He demanded pork and liquor before he would give the loan. He was fond of the heavy, very hot, spiced food cooked in the Bhangi households. Pitaji had borrowed money from him once. He had offered Teja Taga country liquor that day. And pork. Sucking at the pork slices, his face had resembled a spotted dog's. His eyes, red from the drink, looked satanic. His interest rates were so high that one could spend a whole lifetime paying the interest, and the principal would remain untouched. Most residents of the Bhangi *basti* were drowning in debt. So they could not afford to protest too much against any injustice done to them. Most people in our *basti* suffered everything in silence. Honor and prestige had no meaning for them. Being threatened and controlled by the higher-ups was an everyday occurrence for the *basti* dwellers.

Jasbir returned empty-handed from Bagdogra one day. He didn't even have half-decent clothes on his body, let alone money. Despite working all those years for Tirath Ram and Company, he had come back empty-handed. Defeated and tired, he began to do wage labor in the village. The situation of our family was deteriorating rapidly. Meanwhile, Janeswar had also gotten married. Once again we had had to borrow money from Teja Taga for the wedding.

Our mother's brother, Mama, summoned Jasbir to Dehra Dun. Uncle was a sweeper or cleaner in the sanitary department of the Dehra Dun municipality. He also worked at eight or ten homes as a cleaner, removing garbage and cleaning lavatories and sweeping the streets. He had just one son, Surjan. In the beginning Jasbir worked for our uncle. Later he found a permanent job with the Survey of India. Although it didn't pay much, at least it provided some security. A regular income boosts a person's morale. Jasbir began to develop self-confidence after joining the Survey of India.

The days of the rainy season were hellish. The lanes filled up with mud, making walking difficult. The mud was full of pigs' excrement, which would begin to stink after the rain stopped. Flies and mosquitoes thrived and were as thick as clouds of locusts. It became extremely difficult to go outside. Our arms and legs would get smeared with dirt. Our feet became mangy. The spaces between our toes filled up with reddish sores. Once these sores started to itch, they would itch nonstop.

The lanes were full of muddy water for months. The only way to get to school was by crossing these mud-filled lanes. Our area had several ponds, and their water would seep into the lanes. Our *basti* had one well. People had raised money to get it cemented. Both the plinth and the parapet of the well were quite high. Despite this safeguard, the water in the well was full of long worms during the rainy season. We had no alternative but to drink that water. We did not have the right to take water from the well of the Tagas.

It rained a lot in 1962. All the homes of our locality were made of clay. The nonstop rain that fell over many days was disastrous for these clay houses. Our house had sprung leaks all over. We would set a pot under the leak. Every time a drop fell in the pot, it made a sound: tup, tup. We had to stay awake during these rainy nights. The fear that a wall would collapse dogged us constantly. Sometimes a huge hole would suddenly open up in the ceiling, and closing such a hole was a very difficult job. Just climbing up on the roof of the clay houses was a dangerous undertaking.

One night, when it was raining heavily, a big hole opened up in our roof. I was entrusted with the job of going up on the roof because I weighed the least in our family. With the rain pouring down on me, I could see nothing in the pitch dark. Placing my feet on Pitaji's shoulders, I climbed up on the roof. Pitaji guided me from below: "Careful, Munshiji . . . steady feet . . . Don't walk toward the middle . . . Stay near the wall."

I had a big lump of clay in one hand while I groped for the hole with the other in complete darkness. Pitaji called out to me nonstop: "Munshiji, have you found the hole?" At last I succeeded, found the gap, and sealed it with the clod in my hand. I had a hard time climbing down after closing the hole. I could not keep my eyes open in the pouring rain. As I was slowly climbing down, orienting myself by Pitaji's voice, my foot slipped. For a second I felt I was up in the air. But Pitaji's experienced eyes saw me even in that pitch dark, and I managed to regain my balance in his strong grip. My screams brought my mother out, and she was relieved to see me safe. I was shivering from the cold. My mother wiped me dry with a cloth and set me down by the stove.

That night a huge piece of our *baithak* collapsed. Pitaji and Ma did not sleep for a second. Many homes fell down in our *basti*. People were screaming and shouting. Pitaji went out and shouted, "Uncle ... Is everything all right?" Uncle had yelled back in a voice as strong as my father's, "Everything is all right—the back shed has fallen down."

A big commotion started at the crack of dawn in the colony. Everybody was out, looking for a safe place. The rain was continuing to pour. The remaining houses could collapse at any minute. Pitaji went toward the Tagas' houses and he returned shortly. "Hurry up," he called. "I have got the *baithak* of Mamraj opened up." Ma hurriedly gathered up some essentials, and we left for Mamraj Taga's *baithak*, our belongings perched on our heads and our bodies drenched in the rain. Mamraj's *baithak* had been locked up for years. No one used it. Even the plaster on the walls had crumbled. Still, it was a sanctuary.

We hadn't even put our stuff down in Mamraj Taga's *baithak* when another thirty or forty people came in after us. The rest of the people of our neighborhood went somewhere else. Within the blink of an eye, the *baithak* filled up. Stuff was lying all over. The *basti* people brought cooking utensils as well as some other necessities. They had left everything else behind.

A great many people sought shelter in the *baithak*. Our greatest problem was how to light the stove. No one had any fuel. The firewood we had was completely soaked from the rain. We borrowed cow-dung cakes from the Tagas to light a fire. Eight or ten stoves were set up in the *baithak*. Well, there weren't any real stoves.

Three bricks had been put together as makeshift ones. Those who could not find bricks were making do with stones. The smoke rising from these stoves completely transformed the *baithak*. One couldn't even breathe in that smoke. The men had assembled on the veranda and were smoking a hookah. The women were battling with the stoves. The children made such a racket that you could not hear a thing.

As soon as evening fell, the baithak was absolutely dark. No one had a lamp or a lantern. The burning dung cakes in the stoves did not throw enough light to dispel the darkness. Sitting under one roof, people forgot their old grudges. Whatever they had, they wanted to share with others.

Ma boiled yellow split peas that night, with just salt for spice, and that was all we got to eat. The taste of those salted split peas, the feeling of contentment that they provided, has not come my way again, even in five-star hotel food. That night no one cooked dal or vegetable on any stove. Roti, onion, and salt: no one had anything else.

The next day, no one could get a stove lit early. The rain brought us to starvation's door. Life came to a standstill. People were wandering all over the village, hoping to find some grain so that they could light the stove. At such times one couldn't even get a loan [to buy groceries]. Many returned empty-handed after searching all over. Pitaji also returned empty-handed. Hopelessness was writ large on his face. Sagwa Pradhan had laid down his condition for giving grain: indenture a son on an annual lease and take as much grain as you want.

Pitaji had come back without saying a word. But Ma managed to get a few pounds of rice from Mamraj Taga's house and that tided us over. After many days we were going to have a proper meal. Ma put a big pot on the hearth to boil the rice. It did not have much rice, but she had filled it with water right up to the brim. The smell of boiling rice permeated the entire *baithak*. Little children were looking at Ma's stove with expectant eyes.

The water in which the rice has been boiled is called *mar* and

Ma drained it off. She divided that *mar* into two containers. She gave one part a *baghar*, or final flavoring, with hot oil and spices, like dal, and gave each child a bowl of *baghar* and a bowl of *mar*. This *mar* was as good as milk to us. Whenever Ma cooked rice at home, we all got very excited. Our bodies felt energetic after imbibing this hot drink.

The homes of the Julahas, a caste of Muslim weavers, were near our neighborhood. During the marriage season, when the Julahas cooked dal and rice in their homes, the children of our neighborhood ran there with pots in their hands to collect the *mar*. Others threw the *mar* away, but to us it was even more valuable than cow's milk. Many a time the Julahas used to scream at the children to go away. But they stood there shamelessly. The desire to drink the *mar* was more powerful for them than the scolding. The *mar* tasted very nice with salt. And on the few occasions that molasses was available, the *mar* became a delicacy. This taste for *mar* didn't come about because of some trend or fashion. It was due to want and starvation. This thing that everyone discards was a means to quell our hunger.

One day in school Master Sahib was teaching the lesson on Dronacharya. He told us, almost with tears in his eyes, that Dronacharya had fed flour dissolved in water to his famished son, Ashwatthama, in lieu of milk. The whole class responded with great emotion to this story of Dronacharya's dire poverty. This episode was penned by Vyasa, the author of the *Mahabharata*, to highlight Drona's poverty. I had the temerity to stand up and ask Master Sahib a question afterward. So Ashwatthama was given flour mixed in water instead of milk, but what about us who had to drink *mar*, rice water? How come we were never mentioned in any epic? Why didn't an epic poet ever write a word about our lives?

The whole class stared at me as though I had raised a meaningless point. Master Sahib screamed, "Darkest Kaliyug has descended upon us so that an untouchable is daring to talk back."[3]

---

3. The final age, according to the Hindus, is the period called Kaliyug, which is marked by godlessness, strife, and chaos and ends with the destruction of the world.

As a punishment, the teacher ordered me to squat in the *murga*, or rooster position. This meant squatting on my haunches, then drawing my arms through my inner thighs, and pulling down my head to grasp my ears, a painful, constricted position. Instead of carrying on with the lesson, the teacher was going on and on about my being a Chuhra. He ordered a boy to get a long teak stick. "Chuhre ke, you dare compare yourself with Dronacharya. Here, take this, I will write an epic on your body." He had rapidly created an epic on my back with the swishes of his stick. That epic is still inscribed on my back. Reminding me of those hated days of hunger and hopelessness, this epic, composed out of a feudalistic mentality, is inscribed not just on my back but on each nerve of my brain.

I too have felt inside me the flames of Ashwatthama's revenge. They keep on burning inside me to this day. I have struggled for years on end to come out of the dark vaults of my life, powered by little besides the rice water. Our stomachs would get bloated because of a constant diet of this drink. It killed our appetite. It was our cow's milk and it was our gourmet meal. Scorched by this deprived life, the color of my skin has changed.

Literature can only imagine hell. For us the rainy season was a living hell. The epic poets of Hindi have not even touched upon the terrible sufferings of the villages. What a monstrous truth that is.

That year, most of the houses in our *basti* collapsed. It took us months to build them again. No grants or subsidies reached that *basti*. All we could rely on was the strength of our own hands. We rebuilt our ramshackle homes. The same thing happened almost every year. Even the houses that the rains spared suffered considerable damage.

My great-grandfather's name was Zaharia. He had two sons. The elder son's name was Buddha, but everybody called him Buddhu. The younger one was called Kundan. Buddha also had two sons: the elder was Suganchand, and the younger one, my father, was

Chotan Lal. Sugan had only one daughter, who was married off in Paniala village, near Roorki. They lived with her parents.

Chotan Lal had five sons and two daughters. The youngest daughter, Somti, was only two or three years old when she died. Sukhbir was the eldest son. After him came Jagdish, who died when he was eighteen. Next was Jasbir; then came Janesar and then Omprakash, that is, me, the youngest among the brothers. My sister, Maya, is younger than I.

Kundan had three sons: Molhar, Solhar, and Shyamlal. He had two daughters. The elder one was named Choti, and the youngest one was called Shyamo.

Pitaji and his older brother, Suganchand, our *tauji*, were estranged. Once Pitaji took a court paper from an old trunk and showed it to us. It said that Suganchand, son of Buddha, sold the house with the neem tree to Chotan Lal, son of Buddha. The witnesses' signatures were at the bottom, along with the government seal. That is, Pitaji had bought the house we lived in from Tauji, our uncle Sugan. Then what had happened to Pitaji's share of the family property? This question came up again and again in my mind. But I did not dare to ask Pitaji. When I asked Ma, I learned that the house where Tai, our uncle Sugan's wife, lived had been allotted to Pitaji, but she had managed to get possession. This act of hers had caused a permanent schism between our mother and her sister-in-law.

Pitaji and Tauji had a marked resemblance. They had the same height and build, sported the same type of moustache, even had a similar stride. Despite the feud between the two families, we never saw Pitaji and Tauji fighting. The two families made peace at Maya's marriage. I worked very hard to bring that about and was very happy when they reconciled.

The younger *buaji*, our aunt Shyamo, was married in the village of Churiale. Whenever she visited, the home took on a festive appearance. She was the darling of everyone in the family. Pitaji was very fond of his female cousins whom, as is the custom in India, he regarded as sisters and referred to them as such.

Phupaji, our aunt Shyamo's husband, and Pitaji were very close. Pitaji never treated his male and female cousins differently. Pitaji took on the entire expense of his younger cousin's marriage.[4] Afterward, it was Pitaji again who looked after the expenses of Shyamo Bua's *gauna*.[5]

Pitaji's cousin brother Molhar had died suddenly. He would have been about twenty or twenty-two when he died. He was married and the only literate member of the family. Some of his books were lying in an alcove in the front room, wrapped in a piece of cloth. The alcove was high up in the wall. One day I somehow managed to get these books down. They were books of stories in Urdu and Hindi. I put the Urdu books back but read the ones in Hindi. Ma came upon these books one day. She snatched them away from me and hid them somewhere. She was afraid that Molhar's uncle's ghost might start tormenting me.

———

The whole *basti* had strange ideas about ghosts and spirits. If anybody fell sick just a bit, people would call a *bhagat* [sorcerer] instead of a doctor. After the god or the goddess possessed the sorcerer, the sick person would be brought to him. Often this sorcerer possessed by the god would talk about the influence of some ghost or spirit and would act as though he were catching it. In exchange, the gods and the goddesses would be offered pigs, roosters, rams, and liquor. These deities are worshipped in every house. They are different from Hindu deities, and their names won't be found in any *Purana*, even if one searches hard. But go to any family of our clan, and you will find these deities worshipped. Whether it is a birth, a wedding, or a feast for the dead,

———

4. Americans would see her as a mere cousin, but in India, because Chotan regards her as a sister, he feels he has obligations to her that must be met.

5. *Gauna* is the ceremony marking consummation of the marriage, when the young bride is sent to the bridegroom's home; at the time of the wedding the bride may be too young for sexual relations.

nothing can be accomplished without worshipping these deities.

Chachi, our uncle Molhar's wife, had become a widow at a very young age. I was very small then. Now I don't even remember what she looked like. All I remember is that she was pretty. One early morning in winter Ma, my sister-in-law, and Chachi were sitting near the stove. Maya and I were also with them. The fire of cow-dung cake, gave forth heat that was sorely needed. Pitaji and my oldest brother, Sukhbir, had come in from somewhere. They were whispering about something. Suddenly, Pitaji became extremely angry. He picked up a stick lying in the courtyard and struck our aunt's back with it. Chachi doubled up under his blow. A terrified scream came out of her mouth and she clasped my mother. "Save me!" she howled. Pitaji's face was burning with rage. Sukhbir snatched the stick away from him and dragged him outside. The shouting attracted women of the neighborhood who were peeping from their rooftops and walls.

I was too young to understand. But something had happened, something that shook up the whole family. Aunt was sent to her parents' home the same day. Pitaji himself dropped her off at Basera. Because Chachi's native village was Basera, she used to be called "Basero" by everyone.

After this day, even talking about Chachi was banned in our house. What happened caused a great fear to sprout in my mind. The image of Pitaji, who loved his cousins, was replaced in my head by that of a cruel tyrant.

Very soon afterward Ma arranged a match for our uncle Shyamlal. Near Khajuri, my maternal grandparents' village in district Saharanpur, there is a village called Garahu. The river Hinden flows between these two villages. My mother's adopted brother lived in Garahu. He had a daughter named Ramkatori. Mother got Uncle married to her in less than a month. Ramkatori's arrival made us forget the sting of Basero. Shyamlal Chacha also started working day and night after his marriage to Ramkatori.

Then another tragedy occurred. All of a sudden, Shyamlal

Chacha disappeared somewhere. We searched for him everywhere but in vain. Ma asked Ramkatori a lot of questions: "He must have said something before he left?" But Ramkatori had no answers.

After many months Shyamlal Chacha returned in the dark of the night. Immediately after entering the house he attacked his brother Solhar with a knife. Solhar Chacha managed to escape, and Pitaji grabbed Shyamlal Chacha and tied his hands and feet with string. Ramkatori was crouching near Ma. She was terrified.

Shyamlal Chacha lay on the floor, his limbs tied. He called out to Ma, "Bhabhi, untie me—I will never come back here."

Ma untied him although Pitaji forbade her to do so. Shyamlal Chacha left, never to come back.

Pitaji was saddened by what had happened. He had wanted Shyamlal Chacha to stay. He had tried to reason with him: "If something was hurting you, you should have talked to me . . . Why did you take out the knife?"

But Chacha was stubborn. He never showed his face around there. Soon after that Ramkatori took up with Solhar. Relations between the two families became strained after that. All the threads of love binding us had broken apart. It wasn't the same for Ramkatori, either. As long as Pitaji was around the house, she would not come visiting. Our visits to their home were also reduced greatly.

The college [the junior high school called Inter College] was about one and a half miles from the bus stop. There was only one inter college in the vicinity. In addition to the Barla boys, the boys from Fallauda, Mandla, Bhaiani, Khaikheri, Basera, Tajpur, Chapar, Nagla, and Kutubpur also attended this college. Only five or six girls were studying in the college. They were from prosperous families. A couple of girls were the daughters of teachers. Most boys were Tyagis. Only one or two boys from Dalit families studied at the college.

Baburam Tyagi was an inhabitant of Barla. He was a good teacher. I was fortunate to receive his love and guidance. He often encouraged me to participate in debates. He taught us Hindi and helped improve my grasp of the language. The credit for the interest that I developed in Hindi goes to Baburamji. He was a source of inspiration to me in college.

In July or August 1962 I was admitted to class eight.[6] I had passed class seven with good marks. I was one of the four good students of that class. One day I left a bit early for school. Because we did not have a watch or a clock at home, we left for school when we thought it was time. It was early in the morning, and I was perhaps the only one going to school on the paved road. Behind me was Surajbhan Taga's son Brajesh. He was much older than I was. He had a long stick on his shoulder. He was probably going toward his fields. He started to mutter the moment he saw me. I kept walking as though I hadn't heard him. When we got near the Kothi, the building belonging to the irrigation department that was used as a guest house, he called, "Abey, Chuhre ke, stop." The school was not far from there.

I turned to look at him. Mischief was writ large on his face. He came near me and said, "Chuhre ke, you really have sprouted horns. You have become arrogant. Even the way you walk has changed."

When I kept going without replying to him, he came ahead of me, cutting off my escape route. In an angry voice he said, "I hear you are clever in your studies." He planted one end of the stick in my stomach. "Let me also see how bright you are." He was bent on starting a row. I wanted to avoid it. Seeing me quiet, he growled again: "You will remain a Chuhra, however much you study." He pushed me with the stick. I managed to prevent myself from falling, but my bag had fallen on the ground. He picked up the bag, put it on his stick, and twirled it around. I begged him, "My books will be scattered . . . Please return my bag . . . My answer

---

6. The author would have just turned twelve.

books will rip apart." He couldn't care less and, twirling it hard, threw the bag far away. When I ran to pick it up, he started laughing loudly. My bag had fallen into the muddy ditch on the side of the road. My clothes got dirty as I tried to fish it out. My feet were smeared with mud, and the books and notebooks in the bag were soaked. I burst into tears

I washed my hands and feet at the school tap and dried the books and notebooks in the sun. My heart felt very heavy that day. It seemed that studying wasn't going to be possible for me. But Pitaji's face and words kept coming back to me: "You have to improve the caste by studying."

That day I had not been able to concentrate on any lesson. The morning's incident kept tormenting me. After school I told the whole story to my mother and she too started crying. When Pitaji heard the story, he was ready to kill or get killed. Shyamlal Chacha picked up the iron rod. Both wanted to go and beat up that boy. The elders of the *basti* managed to calm them down.

I haven't forgotten Pitaji's hopelessness to this day. "Abey, Sohro [Father-in-law; abuse], if my children learn a few letters, how does it bother you?"

The matter was settled with great difficulty. But now a voice of protest against the Tagas began to emerge in our *basti*. People began to refuse wageless labor. Pitaji would get worked up over little things and start screaming. Ma constantly feared that we might get entangled in some mess.

———

Hiram Singh, Satpal, Bhikuram, and Omi went to school from our *basti*. Satpal and I were the same age. We were admitted together. Hiram was a year behind. Omi dropped out of school. Satpal fell a year behind me. Satpal was a bit weak in his studies. We had been together from childhood. Our homes were also close together. His father, Ghissa, wore a turban like the Sikhs and grew a beard. Their way of speaking also changed. They had named

their children in the Sikh way. The eldest son was named Harnam
Singh, the second was Gurnam Singh, the daughter was Rajinder,
and the youngest was Satnam Singh, who later became Satpal. In
the *basti*, though, he was called Bandar. Similarly, Hiram Singh
was called Sundal, and I was called Paalla. No one in the *basti*
called me Omprakash except my mother. Some people began to
call me Munshiji after my father's nickname for me.

Hiram Singh was married off at about the time he took the
class eight examination. I took the class nine examination that
year. The *barat*, or bridegroom's party, went to Morna. I was in
the wedding party with Pitaji. I was wearing new clothes, and it
was very exciting for me to go with the bridegroom's party. In all
the ceremonies of the marriage, I was the privileged one accom-
panying Hiram. The day after the wedding, before the *vida*, the
departure of the bride to her new home, a man came to the *jan-
wasa* [guest house], where the bridegroom's party had been put
up, to take Hiram to the bride's home. Once again I had to go
with Hiram.

We both sat down on a rope-string cot in the courtyard of the
bride's house. All around us, a bevy of girls was laughing and bantering. I was on my guard because the elders had sent me with
Hiram after imparting many instructions. They had taught me
how to escape the traps laid by these laughing, bantering girls.

The girls were teasing us very hard. They gave us last night's
leftover rice and dal to eat. A man stood with a big drum hanging
from his head. Hiram Singh's mother-in-law and two or three
other women gestured to the drummer to get him started. Hiram
Singh had to go with them to salaam the people at the houses
where his mother-in-law worked.[7] I had tried to stop Hiram
Singh from going to do the salaam, but he did not protest and quietly stood up. I said, "All right, you go, but I am not coming."

---

7. *Salaam* refers to the custom of taking the bride or groom around the neighborhood
to collect donations and presents from the superior castes for whom the Chuhres
provided labor.

But Hiram Singh came and held my hand and said, "Don't leave me in the lurch. Please come with me."

I had a big argument with Hiram Singh for going to do the salaam. But I lost and had to go with him. "Come, *yaar* [great friend]! We will go to a couple of houses and then come back," he had entreated. I went with an uneasy feeling inside.

It was summer. We wandered in the lanes until noon. We were walking as if in a procession. Ahead of us were the bride's mother and two women, behind them the drummer, then me and Hiram Singh, followed by a crowd of children. The shouting of the children drowned out the sound of the drum.

The drummer would stop in front of a house and loudly bang the drum. The girls and the women would come out of the house when they heard it. Hiram Singh would offer his respects or salaam them. The way they looked at him from the corner of their veils, it seemed as if Hiram Singh had been brought from a zoo. Some would behave very roughly and insultingly. The bride's mother had to plead a great deal before anything would be forthcoming. It wasn't easy to get a piece of cloth or a pot from anyone. Hiram's mother-in-law would say, "Chowdhurain, do I have three or four other daughters that any other sons-in-law will come to your door?[1] Please give something so that I can send my daughter away honorably." But this begging of hers did not seem to have much effect.

Some would make a face, saying, "The stomachs of these Chuhras are never filled."

A woman put a one-rupee note on Hiram Singh's palm and said to his mother-in-law, "Arri, your son-in-law is quite handsome. What kind of work does he do?"

Encouraged, she replied, "He is studying . . . He has appeared

---

1. Because the bride does not have sisters, this is the only time her mother will be asking for a gift or donation for a bride.

in the class eight exam." The woman looked at Hiram in surprise. I was standing near him. Examining me from top to bottom, she asked in the same tone, "You . . . study too?"

I nodded my head in affirmation.

"You . . . in which class?"

"I have sat for the ninth's exam."

Her eyes filled with amazement. "You look younger than him."

"Ji, I am younger than him."

She spoke again after some time, "Isn't Barla a Taga town?"

"Ji," I said.

"The Chuhras' progeny also study in the school?" She said in surprise. "Howsoever much you study, you will still remain a Chuhra," she said, taking out her frustration. Then she went back into the house.

The procession went toward the next door. My throat was parched from thirst. My feet were tired from long bouts of standing. I asked the drummer, "Bhaiyya, will you get us some water?"

He looked at me, surprised. "You will get water only when we get home."

All my joy in coming with the bridegroom's party was spoiled. When we returned home drenched in sweat, I drank a huge amount of water. Seeing me drink so much water, the man who was serving us said, "Is there a drought in Barla?"

"No, the salaam has dried up all my water." I have no idea whether that poor illiterate understood my pun. I sat down quietly in a corner to relieve my tiredness. The anguish of wandering from door to door for salaam had completely exhausted me. Something was coming to a boil inside me.

We had had pork and rotis for lunch. Many people had imbibed liquor and they were busy making a ruckus. The others were drowsing on rope cots under the neem tree. In the general mayhem around feeding and seeing off the bridegroom's party, I sat quietly in a corner.

Seeing me sitting by myself, Pitaji had called out, "Munshiji, why are you sitting like that?"

Instead of answering Pitaji's question, I fired off angrily, "Is it right to go for salaam?"

Pitaji stared at me as though he were seeing me for the first time. Seeing him quiet, the restlessness inside me began to pour out. "The bridegroom goes from door to door at his own wedding. It is awful. The bridegrooms of the higher castes don't have to do that. This bride will also go door to door after she arrives in Barla."

Pitaji was listening to me quietly. "Munshiji, sending you to school has been a success. I too have understood your point. We will now break this custom."

Pitaji really broke the custom in our house. My brother Janesar and his wedding guests went to Rajopur, near Luxor. Pitaji refused categorically, saying, "My son will not go salaaming." At my sister's wedding too we did not allow our brother-in-law to go for salaam. We told everybody frankly: whosoever wants to give anything must come here and give it.

It may seem like a simple matter, but whether it is the bride or the bridegroom, this custom creates an inferiority complex in them on the very first day of their marriage. A story that I wrote about salaam—its title was "Salaam"—was published in *Hans* in August 1993. Rajendra Yadav called it a powerful statement on antibrahminism. Caste pride is behind this centuries-old custom. The deep chasm that divides the society is made even deeper by this custom, a conspiracy to trap us in the whirlpool of inferiority. Not just bridegrooms but the brides too often have to endure terrible humiliation. When an illiterate girl from a poor family comes to live among strangers, she is already feeling overwhelmed. Taking her door to door for salaam is excruciatingly painful for her. Many such incidents from my childhood are sprawled inside me, bearing witness to the dark days of the past.

I was in class nine at that time. The financial situation of the family was very bleak. Each member of the family had to work very hard for the sake of a few paise.[2] I never had all the textbooks. I

---

2. One hundred paise equal one rupee; a few cents.

had to get by through borrowing from friends. It was the same story about clothes. I wore whatever I could get. And I ate whatever I was given.

In those days the Chuhras' responsibility was to dispose of dead cattle in the village. As I mentioned earlier, Chuhras had to work without pay for the Tagas, and wherever one worked, the disposal of the employer's dead cattle was a part of the job. No wages were paid for doing this work. Lifting a cow or a buffalo or a bullock required four to six people. The person whose animal had died would be in a great hurry. He would come into the *basti* and shout. He would start swearing if there was a delay. Usually, it took quite some time to collect the group that would pick up the dead animal.

Disposing of a dead animal is a very difficult operation. The front and back legs are tied up and lifted with the help of a thick bamboo pole. For this very hard work the only recompense is curses—what a cruel society we live in, where hard labor has no value. There is a conspiracy to keep us in perpetual poverty.

The dead animal's hide could be sold in the leather market of Muzaffarnagar. One hide would fetch twenty to twenty-five rupees. After paying the wages of the helpers and the traveling expenses, the profit was scarcely ten to fifteen rupees. But even those ten or fifteen rupees seemed a big sum in those days of hardship. The buyer of the hide would fussily examine it for the smallest flaws. If torn or cut, the hide was no good. Salt had to be applied immediately after skinning the animal. Otherwise it spoiled within a day and the buyer rejected it.

One day Brahmdev Taga's bullock fell on the way to the field. It could not get up. Soon after its death Brahmdev came to our house to inform us. Pitaji and my older brother Janesar had gone to a relative's place that day. Only Ma; Maya, my sister; and my eldest sister-in-law, Rahti Devi, were at home. Jasbir was in Dehra Dun with our mother's brother. Mother was worried. Whom could she send to skin the animal? A couple of people were in the *basti* but they did not want to go. Ma talked to Solhar Chacha. He agreed, but he needed someone to accompany him. He would not be able to skin the hide all by himself.

I was in school at that time. Unable to find anyone else, Ma summoned me from school. I had never done this work. Ma's desire was that I should never have to do such work. But she could not afford to lose the ten or fifteen rupees that the sale of the hide would bring. Acknowledging defeat, Ma sent me with Uncle. Solhar was a great shirker. He spent his days playing drums and cards and avoided hard work. Ma was worried that vultures and wild animals might get the dead bullock before we got there.

Chacha started to skin the hide. I helped. Chacha's hand was rather slow. He became tired after a short while and sat down to smoke a *biri*.[3] He handed me a knife and said, "Skin the hide slowly. It will take me the whole day to do it all by myself."

My hands were trembling as I held the knife. I was trapped in a hard place. Chacha taught me how to ply the knife. That day something broke inside me. I skinned the bullock under Uncle's guidance. I felt like I was drowning in a swamp. I was being drawn into the very quagmire that I had tried to escape from. The wounds from the torment that I suffered with Uncle on that hot afternoon are still fresh on my skin.

As the hide was being skinned, the blood inside me was congealing. It took us several hours to skin the hide. Chacha spread the hide on the ground and the dry soil absorbed its blood. He then tied the hide in a sheet and carried the bundle on his head. Our home was about two miles away. Uncle had to walk fast because of the weight. Knife in hand, I was almost running behind him. We took the paved road to Basera, and soon we were getting close to the bus terminal. Chacha set the bundle down and said, "Now you take it from here. I am tired."

I pleaded with Uncle but it was no use. "Chacha, get me past the bus terminal crowd. The school is about to close. If my classmates see me carrying this bundle, they will bug me in school," I

---

3. A *biri* is an Indian cigarette, raw tobacco wrapped tightly around a piece of *sal* leaf.

begged him in a weepy, tear-filled voice. But he would not relent. He put the bundle on my head. Because there was no way out, I carried it somehow. The weight of the bundle was way beyond my capacity. Only my heart knows how I made my way out of the throng of familiar faces at the bus terminal that day. A fear was constantly tugging at me—what if someone saw me? What if I bumped into a fellow student? If someone started to ask me, what would I say? By the time we reached home, my legs had given up. I felt like I was going to fall at any second. We had to make a long circle around the village to get to the *basti*.

Ma burst out crying when she saw the state I was in. I was covered in muck from head to toe. Bloodstains were clearly visible on my clothes. My eldest sister-in-law said to my mother, "Don't make him do that work. We can bear hunger. Don't drag him in this dirt." Those words of Bhabhi shine like a light in darkness for me to this day. I have come out of that dirt, but millions are living that horrible life even today.

The next day Hiram Singh and I had to take the hide to the city. Pitaji and Janesar had not come back. Hiram Singh's family used to take animal skins and bones to the city and sell them there. I hid the hide under the seat in the tonga, a horse-drawn carriage for hire, so that the other passengers would not notice it. The conductor would not let us get into the bus. Hiram Singh had arranged the trip with a tonga that had a Muslim driver. The *tongawala*, or driver, let the other passengers off in front of the hospital and then took us to the leather market.

Piles of leather were lying everywhere in the leather market. Stench-laden gusts were blowing from the direction of the godowns of dry bones. It was awful to breathe that foul air. The hide fetched twenty-five rupees. The tonga driver took two of them.

We got home before dark. When I gave Ma the money, she gave it back to me. "You don't have textbooks. Whatever books this money can buy, buy them. I will somehow manage."

I said to Ma, "Give some money to Chacha out of this." Ma

scolded me, "Don't take his name in front of me. Let your father come, I will have him thrashed."

Ma was furious with Uncle, who also avoided any contact with her that day. Chacha respected Ma. And Ma, howsoever bitterly she spoke, was fond of both *chachas*, Solhar and Shyamlal. She used to get very unhappy because of their lousy work habits, but she would stand alongside them during their hour of need. Though they were Pitaji's cousins, Ma considered them his siblings.

I have inherited this closeness to family ties from Pitaji. All of a sudden one day Ma's brother arrived in Barla with his son, Surjan, in tow. He said to Ma, "He must no longer live in Dehra Dun. He has fallen into bad company. Get him admitted to school here."

Surjan was admitted into class nine. Surjan and I were together in class nine, in the same section.

Janesar had cataracts in both eyes. He was very perturbed. For a long time he tried home remedies. But instead of improving, his eyesight continued to deteriorate. An eye clinic that offered free treatment came to the village. Janesar was admitted to the clinic for treatment and had eye surgery. His eyes were not yet fully healed, and Surjan used to change his bandages and put medicine in his eyes. Surjan and Janesar almost got arrested while he was recuperating.

What happened was that the young men of the *basti* had refused to work without wages. In the beginning, instead of refusing flat-out, they would try to stall and make some excuse or other. The older men did not know how to refuse straight out.

The Tagas realized that we were slipping from their control. Therefore the moment one of us demanded wages, they would get hopping mad. They were looking for a way to maintain their domination without changing anything. They had the help of the chief

constable of Purkazi police station, who belonged to their caste.
He was looking for an occasion, and, like ripe fruit, it suddenly fell
into his hand.

The government's irrigation department owns a building that
is used as a guest house for visiting dignitaries. On the road that
goes from the bus terminal to Muzaffarnagar, before the college,
there is an old building with faded yellow and red paint; it stands
in a clump of trees. The building is divided into many parts. Once
upon a time, when British officers went on tour, they stayed in this
building, which the villagers call the *kothi* [a substantial house]. All
around the building are fields laden with waving crops. In front of
it is the tarred road.

The land was being surveyed in the village. Some high-ranking officer was coming. As always, a government employee came to
the Bhangi *basti*. The surveyors needed some people for clean-up
work, for which they would not be paid. As always, it would be
unpaid labor. For days on end hungry and thirsty people would
work to clean the *kothi*. In return they would be sworn at. Police
constables would forcibly take poultry away from the *basti*. There
was no place to make a complaint; instead, some Tagas would
cooperate with the police in this robbery. The moment they saw
the police, the women of the *basti* would hide inside their homes.

This time around, the *basti* folk refused to work without being
paid. We will go if you pay us daily wages, they said, and that led
to a row. The man who had come to call them for work was an
employee of the lowest rank of the district government, but his
manner was no less domineering than that of a high-ranking officer. He swore at us in every sentence. When everybody refused to
go, he resorted to arm twisting. But everybody disappeared, one by
one, and he had to leave empty-handed.

Before leaving, he made threats.

Fifteen days after this event two constables came to the *basti*
and took ten people with them. They grabbed whoever happened
to cross their path. Janesar's eyes were bandaged. Surjan went
inside immediately, or he too would have been trapped. I was not

in the *basti* at that time. I returned after the police had come and gone. I learned that the police had taken away Baru, Dhannu, Mamchand, and some others.

Ilias had a garden in front of his cowshed, near the road. Across the road was the office of the Panchayat, or local government.[4] Ilias was sitting in the garden on a rope-string cot, smoking a hookah. He held a ruler, which he constantly flourished. Eight or ten police were standing around, batons in hand, guns strapped to their shoulders. They were making the arrestees squat like a rooster and a policeman was beating them with a baton. The policeman who was beating them was getting tired. The one being beaten would scream after every blow. This festival of valor was being celebrated openly. People watched quietly, without a word. No one protested.

The women and children of the *basti* were standing in the lane and crying loudly. The police had arrested their men for no reason. They could not think of what else they could do but cry. The *basti*'s leaders, Kirpa and Ghissa, had gone to see the village chief, the *pradhan*, and had not returned yet. We found out afterward that the *pradhan* had left for the city on the pretext of some important work just as the police raided our *basti*.

No one in the *basti* had the courage to ask the head constable why these people were being beaten. What crime had they committed?

This farce went on for an hour. All ten men who had been beaten were groaning with pain. Their screams had made the birds in the trees take off, but paralysis had struck the villagers, who could not express their empathy. My mind was filled with a deep revulsion. I was then an adolescent, and a scratch appeared on my mind like a line scratched on glass. It remains there still. The poem by Sumitranandan Pant that we had been taught at school, "Ah, how wonderful is this village life"—each word of the poem had proved to be artificial and a lie. What happened that day caused a

---

4. Ilias was a villager, and his name indicates that he was probably a Muslim.

storm inside me. Perhaps the seeds of Dalit poetry were germinating inside, preparing to sprout at the right time. It was experiences like these that made me write the poem "Thakur ka Kuan" (The Thakur's Well).

I have not been able to forget these bitter memories. They flash in my mind like lightning every now and then. Why is it a crime to ask to be paid for one's labor? Those who keep singing the glories of democracy use the government machinery to quell the blood flowing in our veins. As though we are not citizens of this country. They have suppressed the weak and the helpless for thousands of years, just in this manner. No one will ever know how many talents their deception and treachery have wiped out.

Those people returned home after a severe beating, bereft of all hope. Silence was glued to their faces. Their eyes held deep anguish. Their bodies were wounded. That day no one lit a stove in the *basti*. Everyone was apprehensive. This tragedy put an end to all camaraderie. Then began a series of departures from the village. Dhannu, Harnam, Gurnam, Fauza, Jasbir —one after the other they took off for the city where a new brightness was beckoning. When the earth of the village becomes barren, one no longer has the desire to irrigate and fertilize it. When one's village is no longer one's own, nothing to lose in leaving.

———

When anybody got sick in the *basti*, instead of treating them with medicine, people tried things like tying threads, talismans, using spells, and so on to get rid of the evil spirit, which was deemed to be the cause of the illness. All such ceremonies were performed at night. When the disease was prolonged or became serious, then a *bhagat*, who, as I mentioned earlier, was a kind of sorcerer, would perform *puchha*, or exorcism. He would be accompanied by a drummer who played the *dholak*, an oval-shaped drum that hung in front from his shoulders, and two or three singers. They sang to the beat of the drum. Their song was an invitation to the *devta,* or god, who would enter the body of the sorcerer and make him sway. The singing, the beat, and the drumming created such an atmosphere that even a rational person would start swaying. The songs were full of vulgar expressions, a mark of familiarity toward the god.

The singing and the drumming stopped the moment the sorcerer began to sway. The moment the sorcerer's head or hand swayed, it was considered a sign of the spirit's arrival. The spirit told its name, greeted everybody. And then an elderly family member described the patient's disease to the spirit. The spirit touched the patient and then prescribed that the evil spirit had to be appeased.

Kalwa and Hari Singh Nalwa are very special spirits and are worshipped widely. There are many *devis,* or goddesses, as well. Mai Madaran is among the most important.

Although the *basti* people were Hindus in name, they did not worship any Hindu gods or goddesses. At Janmashtami, the birth anniversary of Lord Krishna, they do not worship Krishna but Jaharpir, another god. Or they worship the spirits. And not on eighth day, the *ashtami,* but on the morning of the ninth day of worship, the *navami.* In the same way, during the Deepawali [festival] it is not the goddess Lakshmi but Mai Madaran who is worshipped and offered a piglet. Or halvah and *pooris* are prepared as offerings.

Whatever the festival, people worship particular gods and goddesses. After the exorcism the god overpowers the evil spirit and orders it to set the patient free. Afterward the wishes of the god are fulfilled. A pig is sacrificed and a bottle of liquor offered.

Whether it is a wedding or a birth or a death, worshipping the gods is essential. If someone forgets, or skips this step, something terrible might happen to that person. Even though I grew up in this atmosphere, after reaching the age of discernment, I never had any faith in these gods and goddesses. The sorcerer seemed a pretender to me. Whenever my family performed these *pujas,* or religious ceremonies, I would either sit outside or wander around. I started avoiding the *puja* early on. Pitaji would get upset with me.

He would talk about the beliefs of the ancestors, but that didn't work with me. I did not argue with him about these issues but sat quietly. He would get irritated and scold me. Afterward, frustrated, he too would become quiet. He would ask repeatedly, "Munshiji . . . I hope you haven't become a Christian." I would reassure him, "No, no. I haven't become a Christian."

But something came to a boil inside me, and I wanted to say, "Neither am I a Hindu." If I really were a Hindu, would the Hindus hate me so much? Or discriminate against me? Or try to fill me up with caste inferiority over the smallest things? I also wondered why one had to be a Hindu in order to be a good human being—I have seen and suffered the cruelty of Hindus since childhood. Why does caste superiority and caste pride attack only the weak? Why are Hindus so cruel, so heartless against Dalits?

After scolding me, Pitaji would get busy with the ceremony. All the family members would have gathered there. I would be alone, lost in myself, looking for myself in the deep layers of darkness. I became quiet and introverted.

In the quiet of the night, whenever I heard the drum that summoned the spirits and the songs in some neighboring house, I could not fall asleep. When the process of making someone a sorcerer started, the drum would play and the singing would go on for a month and a quarter.

For five weeks an oil lamp would burn in the house, and the person who was becoming a sorcerer would stand in front of it with folded hands and concentrate. He wore a thick necklace made of thread. Someone would keep throwing incense on coals kept near the lamp, and its smoke created a mysterious atmosphere as it wafted all over the house. The guru invoked the god who was tempted by all sorts of offerings in order to persuade him to manifest himself in a new sorcerer's body. Many a person did not manage to become a sorcerer even after a whole month's observances. Those who were successful offered liquor and a pig to the god. The whole *basti* was invited to a meal. The sorcerer could now conduct exorcism at anybody's house.

Burja's house was near ours. His body used to receive the god Badi. At such times he used to emit several types of sounds from his mouth. He would jump around and do somersaults. At such times the *basti* atmosphere was frightening. Children were forbidden to leave the house after sundown. Everybody felt as though ghosts were hovering all over.

Whereas I rejected the existence of ghosts rationally, deep inside I was culturally conditioned to fear them. It took me a long time to free myself of this fear. During the summer holidays I went to Dehra Dun for a month. But as soon as I got there, I fell ill with dysentery, which took a long time to recover from. I returned to the village before the school reopened. I would get stomach cramps and my stomach ached all the time. Pitaji took me to a couple of quacks, but my condition did not improve. I became very weak. I was quite skinny to begin with and the dysentery made me even thinner.

In the meantime a distant brother-in-law of mine from Kendki visited us. He was a sorcerer. Pitaji told him about my health problems. He examined me and told Pitaji, "Why do you bother about doctors and medicines? He has become possessed by a spirit." He squatted on the floor and began to mumble something. Then, suddenly, his whole body began to shake. He asked for a piece of cloth. He made a whip from it. A very frightening sound came out of his mouth. The whip flashed in the air and landed on my back. I was already weak and on top of that to be hit by a whip! I became enraged. When he waved the whip again, I tried to stop it, crying, "Jija, what are you doing? It hurts!" But he wasn't listening. He kept on whipping me. Finally, I snatched the whip away from his hands. He began to frighten me in an even louder voice. I shouted and called out to Pitaji, "He will kill me if you don't stop him. I don't have any spirit sticking to me."

Suddenly, his god or spirit disappeared from his body. He sat quietly, holding his head in his hands. Every inch of my body ached. When none of his tricks worked on me, he left for his village the next morning.

My opinion about all these things being a fraud was strength-
ened. Who knows how many people these sorcerers have killed?
Two of my brothers died without any proper treatment or medication. Jagdish, who was so strong, was hardly seventeen or eighteen at the time of his death. He had died after a two-day fever.
Sukhbir was about twenty-four or twenty-five when he died.
Every year a couple of deaths occurred in the *basti* in this way. Even
then people's faith in these gods and sorcerers did not diminish.

The pig killed for the ceremony of worship and the liquor created a festive atmosphere. Two swallows and a man began to fly.
The liquor was homemade and very strong. Once in a while country liquor would be brought from Chapar's or Purkazi's liquor
store. It was quite common to quarrel, swear, and get violent after
drinking the liquor. Even little things got exaggerated, and people
ended up with bashed heads.

Such was life. These were important times for me. In those
days I wanted to run away from them. Today, they are my strength.
They provide me solace.

———

On the western edge of the village, on the bank of a large pond,
was a temple of the goddess Mata on a high platform. The pond
was full of water lilies. Once upon a time this temple was under a
huge banyan tree that was surrounded on three sides by the homes
of the Tagas. In the month of Asharh, which fell between mid-June
and mid-July, a special ceremony of worship, or *puja*, was performed in the temple. The *basti* people united avidly for this annual *puja*. The *basti* people themselves brought the offerings for the
puja. There would be clothes; *chunariyas*, or long flimsy scarves;
bangles; coins; food, like *pooris*, *malpuas* [dessert pancakes], halvah,
batashas [round white candies]; sometimes a silver ring. There
would be violent fights over the distribution of these offerings.

Women and children from nearby villages came to the temple
in bullock carts to fulfill their pledges. People had boundless faith

in the temple deity. The *basti* people pounced on the temple offerings like vultures. The elders of the village got together and found
a way to avoid these disputes: three or four people would collect
the temple offerings and then distribute them in the *basti*. When
this decision was implemented, for the first time a mountain of
delicacies—*pooris* and *malpuas*—came our way.

Mata *puja* was important for *basti* people for another reason.
One tradition was to offer piglets, cocks, and rams to the Mata.
Every house in the *basti* raised poultry and pigs for this occasion.
It was a way of making a little money, a little bit of relief from
dire need.

That year we had eight or ten piglets in our home, and we
managed to sell most of them. All the members of the household
were busy. Pitaji and Janesar were busy all morning, killing and
cleaning and cutting up the piglets. A customer suddenly arrived
from Khaikheri. He bought a piglet without haggling. But he had
to sacrifice the piglet in the garden opposite the temple where
other members of his family were staying. Pitaji and Janesar were
unable to go because they had so much to do at home.

Pitaji tied up the mouth and feet of the piglet with a cord. Even then a screeching sound was coming from its mouth. The school was closed that day. I had to help Pitaji and Janesar in their work. Pitaji put the tied-up piglet on my shoulder. I looked at him in amazement, but Pitaji forced me to go with the customer. He was angry with me for hesitating.

I found it hard to walk with an eight- or ten-kilo piglet on my shoulders. The man walked ahead of me at a fast space. I was hampered by the piglet's weight and kept falling behind. The garden was quite far from home, and by the time we got there my hands and feet had become numb. Many bullock carts were standing there. Some women were singing songs of the Mata, accompanied by a drum. Some people had gathered around a hookah. The children were absorbed in their games.

The moment they heard the screeching of the piglet, the children crowded around me, abandoning their games. They were fascinated by the tied-up piglet. The man called his wife, and she came with some rice and turmeric in a *thali*, a round platter. A woman had smeared the floor with cow dung, and another one had drawn a square on it with flour. The man put the piglet on the square. His wife touched its ears and forehead with turmeric and rice and loudly said, "Mata ki jai!" which everyone present repeated loudly. The man said to me, "Here, take the knife and begin . . . with Mata's name." These moments were no less than a horrifying blast for me. I had never done this work, though I had seen Pitaji doing it. Nonetheless, I found these tasks repulsive. My hands were shaking.

Seeing me standing quietly, the man roared, "Hey, why don't you start?"

I said to him, "You do it yourself. I won't be able to."

"I can't do it—what do you mean? I have given you the money. You will have to do it." There was anger in his eyes. I tried to prepare myself, but I could not gather the courage. The man roared again.

With trembling hands I put the knife in the piglet's chest and pressed. It screamed loudly. My eyes had closed. When I increased the pressure a bit, the knife went in about an inch, and a fountain of blood erupted. The man shouted, "Go in farther." But the knife would not go in any deeper. The man took hold of the handle and increased the pressure.

My clothes, hands, face—all were sprayed with blood. Though the knife had penetrated its heart, the piglet had not died. Stupefied, I held on to the knife that had plunged into its heart.

When it still did not die, those people had put it on the fire. The piglet had screamed the moment it felt the heat. At that moment I had felt as though blisters had erupted all over my body. Suddenly, I ran away from that place. I drew breath only after I reached home. Pitaji was still busy with a customer. Before he could ask me anything, I went inside to Ma. When she saw the condition I was in, she panicked. Lying in Ma's lap, I burst out sobbing. If Ma had not looked after me that day, I think the blood vessels in my brain would have burst. The vortex of pain and disgust that I was caught up in at that moment had soiled my innermost self.

Ma and Pitaji had a big fight about this. It came to blows. Ma declared unequivocally, "Omprakash will not do this work." Pitaji stormed out angrily. Perhaps he went to the place that I had run away from, leaving the job half done. "I have taken their money and I must deliver" was his perspective. It was a matter of keeping his word.

I felt strained for many days afterward.

Tyagi Inter College was outside the village. A hillock beside the tarred road to Muzaffarnagar had been leveled to build the college. Now the name of this college is Barla Inter College, Barla. Surrounding it on all sides are waving green fields. Barla Village is toward the north of the college and Chapar is to its south, Tajpur to its east and Nagla to its west. The majestic building of the college, with its two circular ends, is attractive. The back of the building is shaped like the letter E of the English alphabet. In the beginning it was a one-story building. The second story was built later. The college was airy and pleasant, especially during winter when classes were held outside in the sun.

The playground was very large. In front of the building was a big, pleasantly green compound. Every day, before the beginning of classes, everyone assembled in the compound for prayer. A flag was hoisted there on August 15, Independence Day, and on January 26, Republic Day. The students formed lines to stand before the flag and pray.

Phool Singh Tyagi was the physical education teacher. He was hot tempered and vulgar tongued. His nose would be out of joint at all times. He swore at every little thing. He was constantly picking at his teeth with a wooden pick. Besides phys ed, sometimes he would also teach us Hindi. Rather, he made us memorize it. He was in charge of the National Cadet Corps as well. All the students were in mortal fear of him. Our fear of him pursued us like our shadow.

He terrorized the students the moment he entered the class. If anybody stirred even a little bit in the class, he would be made to squat in the painfully contorted position of a rooster for hours. Slaps and kicks were common. We were afraid even to stand near him. We never could tell when his hands or legs would begin to move. We were all very scared of him. One day he was angrier than usual at prayer time. The monitor of our class, Ram Singh, was standing at the front of the row. I was behind him, and behind me was Surjan Singh, who was the son of my mother's brother. He was many years my senior in age, but we became classmates in class nine. On the right of our row stood the class ten students who were very mischievous. Ram Singh told them to behave themselves. Phool Singh Tyagi stood in front, with the teachers. He thought that Ram Singh was up to some mischief. He screamed at Ram Singh, "Abey, Kala Daroga [Black Sergeant, his derogatory name for Ram Singh], stand up straight or else I will make you crooked with my stick."[1]

A loud burst of collective laughter erupted when he called Ram Singh "Kala Daroga." This made Phool Singh even more irate. Although the whole crowd had laughed, Phool Singh went for Surjan Singh, who was standing behind me. He kicked and slapped Surjan Singh mercilessly. It didn't seem like a teacher who was punishing his student. Rather, it seemed like a hoodlum was roughing up an innocent victim. Surjan Singh fell to the ground, and Phool Singh was kicking and belting him nonstop.

A comment he made that day is still etched in my mind like a scratch on glass: "Abey brother-in-law, progeny of a Chuhra, let me know when you die. You think you are a hero. Today I will beat you till there is nothing left."

Phool Singh had tired of beating Surjan Singh, who was lying on the ground, his face puffed up, his body blue all over. All the students were standing dazed. The teachers were watching the spectacle quietly. The principal, Yashvir Singh Tyagi, stood quietly too. No one protested or retaliated. Every follicle on my body was trembling with fear. My heart was filled with terror. It seemed like all my blood had been drained out. After this incident I often had nightmares. I constantly felt scared. I became introspective and did not feel like talking to anybody.

Whatever effect the beating had on Surjan Singh, this inhumane act remains fresh in my memory. The same terror overtakes my consciousness when I think of that day. Surjan Singh had not

---

1. Students in class nine are around fifteen years old. "Black sergeant" was something Phool Singh thought up to insult Ram Singh, who had a dark complexion. A *daroga*, or sergeant, keeps the junior policemen in order.

done anything and yet he was beaten up. If laughing was a crime, we had all laughed. Then why was only Surjan Singh punished?

Surjan Singh was in trouble all the time at school. He had lived in Dehra Dun since his childhood. His manners and dress were not only different, they were superior. They all minded that. Teachers and classmates, they all disliked him for that. How dare he be superior to them? He was born in a Chuhra home!

After the beating Surjan Singh lost interest in his studies. He returned to Dehra Dun immediately after taking the high school board exams. Now he wanted to take revenge against Phool Singh. But he was in no position to act on it. The passage of time reduced the pain of his wound.

Such were the model teachers that I had to deal with. Moving from childhood to adolescence, when my personality was being shaped, I had to live in this terror-filled environment. How will those who have never suffered the needle pricks of hatred and jealousy feel my pain? Who have never endured humiliation? How will they know what it feels like? Dreams, like sand dunes, do not make a sound when shattered.

At times I feel like I grew up in a cruel and barbaric civilization.

Brajpal Singh Tyagi joined Inter College as a teacher right after receiving his bachelor of science degree. He was our science teacher. He was from a village near Devband and he had many relatives in Barla. He bought a green bicycle soon after his appointment. In those days few people had bicycles. The college principal, Yashvir Singh Tyagi, also came to the college on a bicycle.

I had learned to bike on a rented bicycle. I fell many times and got hurt, but I was obsessed with bicycling. Mango orchards near our *basti* served as our playgrounds as well as camps for marriage parties. The school where I got my primary education, which was started by Sewak Ram Masihi, was held in one of these mango orchards, and I learned to bike there. These orchards have been cut down to build houses, but I still hoard a lot of memories related to my life there.

Two brothers named Balakram and Bhikhuram lived in the *basti*. The elder one, Balakram, was a sweeper at the Inter College. The younger, Bhikhuram, helped him. The principal gave Bhikhuram permission to sit in on the class. He had no formal education. He was eight or nine years older than his classmates. He studied diligently. He would also run errands for college teachers.

One day he said that he had to go to the village of Master Brajpal. He had to bring a sack of wheat from his home, and he wanted me to accompany him. I asked him where was he going to get a bicycle. He said, "We will go on Master Brajpal's bike." I became excited when I heard that we were going to take the teacher's green bike.

When I asked Pitaji's permission, he said yes, and we left the next morning. The road from Barla to Devband was unpaved and it was very hard to bike on it. In some places we encountered so much sand that we found it hard to drag the cycle through it. After passing the little creek past Gupali, we came to the banks of the Kali River. Bhikhuram lifted the bicycle on his shoulder while crossing the river. From Devband we had about two miles of paved road and then it was dirt road up to the village. Bhikhuram gave me the cycle when we came to the paved road. He sat on the carrier; Bhikhuram was quite heavy, but in my eagerness to ride the cycle, I overlooked his weight.

We reached Brajpal Singh's village before the sun came up. When we reached his house, the men had already left for the fields, and only the women and the children were at home. Brajpal Singh's brother arrived after we had waited for a long time. He took Bhikhuram inside, probably to the granary, while I sat on the porch outside. We had parked the bicycle in the lane below.

An elder came in after some time. He lay down on the rope-string cot on the porch, using as a pillow a cloth that he had on his shoulder. He was quite thin; his facial bones jutted out. He called out for somebody, and Brajpal Singh's brother came out. When he started to take away the cold *chillum*, or bowl from the hookah, the elder asked, "Who is that?" He was pointing at me.

"He has come from Barla, Brajpal has sent him . . . They have come to fetch the wheat. One of them is inside, filling the wheat in the sack," the brother replied.

The elder looked at me and said, "Son, why are you sitting there? . . . Come, sit on the cot with me."

"Babaji, I am quite fine here," I replied.

"No, son, come, sit here," When he insisted, I got up and sat on the cot.

"Have you had some education?" the elder asked.

"Yes, I am in the tenth."

"My Brajpal teaches you?"

"Ji."

The elder became quiet. After a while he said, "My Birajpal was getting a collectorship.[2] He didn't want it. He was adamant, 'I want to be a teacher. The country lacks good teachers.' I also said, 'Do whatever you want. Don't worry about here. There is plenty of ancestral land.'"

I was listening to his monologue. He went on talking—about himself, about his family. As though that was all there was in the world. Nothing beyond it.

Brajpal Singh's brother came out and said, "Come, food is ready. Come, eat." When I refused, he said, "If you leave without eating, what will they say about us in Barla?"

I rose halfheartedly when he kept on insisting. I was in a strange frame of mind. After crossing the porch I came to an open courtyard, which was surrounded by brick houses. Each house had a front veranda. On one veranda were two brass platters, on a floor plastered with cow dung. Underneath the platters a big pebble had been placed on one side. The platters held molasses and pickles. Brajpal's brother asked Bhikhuram and me to sit down. Deeply

---

2. A collectorship is a prestigious post in the district administration.

afraid, I sat down. Hesitation and fear were oppressing me together. The mystery of the pebble beneath the platter was cleared up when a thin dal was poured in. The pebble had been placed so that the dal would not spread all over the platter. The aroma of the hot rotis traveled through my nostrils down to my lungs. For me it was the first time that I had sat down to eat in this manner and in a Taga's home. He was feeding us very attentively, but I remained apprehensive. Bhikhuram had eaten a lot of rotis, but I was finding it hard to eat.

Somehow we finished the meal and came out. Bhikhuram sat down on the cot next to the elder's. I was standing at a short distance. In the meantime someone else had arrived. The elder extended the hookah pipe to him. As he drew on the hookah, the man asked the elder about us. The moment he heard that we had come from Barla, he fired a question, "What is your caste?"

I answered his question, "We are of the Chuhra caste."

Both exclaimed together, "Chuhra?" Lifting a heavy stick from beneath the cot, the elder hit Bhikhuram on his back. The old man had a lot of strength and Bhikhuram crumbled. Obscenities began to rain from the elder's mouth. His eyes were fierce and his skinny body was harboring the devil. We had dared to eat from their dishes and sit on their cots, a crime in his eyes. I was standing below the porch, frightened. The elder was screaming, and his voice drew a crowd. Many people suggested that we should be tied to a rope and hung from a tree.

Brajpal Singh's brother tried to calm the elder down, and the elder swore at him too. The hollowness of their hospitality was exposed. Respect depends on the guest's caste. How did we have any entitlement to hospitality? My apprehensions turned out to be correct. Somehow we managed to escape their wrath.

We had the sack of wheat. After loading it on the cycle, we left the village. We were both silent. We had to push the cycle on the unpaved road. We rode on the bike the moment we got on the paved road. Bhikhuram was very angry with me. He felt that I was responsible for the whole fiasco. Why did I have to tell the truth?

Lying had gotten us wonderful food and respect. My truth telling had resulted in a beating and insults.

The cuts that I have received in the name of caste—even eons won't suffice to heal them. Every pedal on the cycle felt heavy as a ton. Instead of taking the unpaved path from Devband, we took the circuitous but paved route: Rohana, Rampur Tiraha, Chapar, and on to Barla. The route was longer but the road was paved. The bicycle had to carry the wheat and the weight of the two of us. We stopped to rest on the Bavan Dare Bridge on the Kali River. Up to that point Bhikhuram was riding the bike. After the bridge it was my turn. Bhikhu sat on the bar in the front. Evening was about to fall. We wanted to reach Barla before it got dark.

But adversity befell us. A pedestrian collided with our bike. I lost my balance and both of us fell, along with the bike. We weren't hurt, but a bullock cart's wheel crushed the cycle's front wheel. The rim and front spoke were twisted badly. The accident was so sudden that we were surprised. We stood there hopelessly, looking at the bicycle.

There were no shops nearby. A rickshaw puller was coming with an empty rickshaw. We put the cycle and the sack of wheat in it and sat down. I didn't have a single paisa; whatever Bhikhu had, he gave the rickshaw puller, who left us in the Muzaffarnagar bazaar at a bicycle repair shop. The repairman assured us that he would straighten the rim and spoke, but he increased our troubles by saying that the bike would not be able to carry both of us. We stared at each other. We pacified the repairman by giving him five kilos of wheat. Our pockets were empty.

It was night. It would have been hard to walk to the village. We went toward the bus terminal with the cycle and the wheat. The last bus was still there and a big crowd was around it. We had thought that we would be able to borrow the fare from an acquaintance, but we did not see anyone we knew.

Bhikhuram remembered Master Vedpal Tyagi, who had left teaching and become a clerk for the bus company. Leaving me at the terminal, Bhikhuram went looking for him. By chance he found him.

But there was no room in the bus. Only one of us could somehow get on. Bhikhuram put the cycle and the sack on the roof of the bus and was getting into the bus when I asked him, "How will I get back?"

"I have to go. You come on the morning bus. Master Vedpal is sitting in the office. He will put you on the bus tomorrow morning." Before I could say anything to Bhikhuram, the conductor blew the whistle. The sound that the bus made drowned out my voice. I was left standing in the bus terminal, which had begun to empty as soon as the last bus left. I didn't have a single paisa in my pocket. Nor did I know anyone in the city. I was in big trouble. I walked toward the booking office. I peeped into a room where Master Vedpal was tallying the accounts. He had been a teacher in Tyagi Inter College. Gathering my courage, I said to him, "Master Sahib, Bhikhuram has left. I was with him . . ." He gestured to me to wait and kept on working on his accounts. I kept waiting for him, standing near the door.

He came out after a very long time. "Let's go. I will put you on the first bus tomorrow morning."

I spluttered, "Masab, I don't have the money for the fare."

He gestured for me to come with him. I walked behind him. I was feeling weak and frightened. He took me to a tea stall and ordered a cup of tea and a bun for me. For himself he ordered milk. At that moment that cup of tea and a bun were no less than gourmet delicacies for me. I was hungry, but my fear and the pain of being left alone in the city killed my hunger.

His little room had two rope cots. Some clothes hung on hooks on the wall. The room had no other furniture. "Go, lie down on that cot. I will put you on the six o'clock bus in the morning," he reassured me. He had probably guessed how frightened I was.

I didn't even feel the ropes on the bare cot. After changing, Master Vedpal stretched out on the other cot. It was not more than ten or fifteen minutes when someone called. Master Vedpal opened the door. A man and a woman were standing outside. Vedpal called them in. The woman entered the room. I too got up and sat quietly. The woman stood quietly in a corner while Vedpal and her companion were whispering on the veranda. After some time Vedpal picked up his cot and put it on the veranda. He asked me to come out as well. "It's just for the night. Lie down on the floor. These people have come unannounced." I lay down on the veranda on the bare floor. Sleep had vanished. There were a lot of mosquitoes.

Vedpal lay down on the cot. Those two were inside. After some time strange noises began to come from inside. The cot too was making a loud creaking sound. I was trying to understand the significance of these sounds. After some time it became quiet. That man came out of the room. Sitting down on Vedpal's cot, he said, "It is a great consignment. Go, have fun." He lit a biri.

Vedpal went into the room. After a short while those strange noises started again. My breathing became rapid, and I was beginning to sense what was happening. My body stiffened, but I remained on the floor, pretending to be asleep. Those people thought that I was asleep. Along with the shallow breathing and grunts like those of a wild animal, the rhythmic creaking of the cot was pointing to a special activity indulged in by men and women, an activity that was still a mystery to me.

The sounds stopped. Vedpal came out. Both of them were cracking vulgar jokes. The man pointed toward me. "Who is this boy? Send him in too. He too will get a taste." Both of them laughed out loud. I held my breath.

The whole night went on that way. Sometimes Vedpal was in and sometimes his friend. How that woman felt about it, I could not even imagine at that time. I could not see what was going on inside the room because one of the men was always outside. When I think of that woman today, I begin to feel nauseated. What helplessness had brought her to them? Did she come willingly? A woman surrendering to two men—even today my mind refuses to accept it.

At five in the morning Master Vedpal brought me to the bus terminal. He put me on the first bus.

I had to face Pitaji's anger the moment I reached home. Bhikhuram had told him the whole story the night before.

The night that I spent on Vedpal's veranda disturbed me a great deal. Besides, I was deeply scared about the condition of Brajpal Singh's brand new bicycle. I had asked Bhikhuram not to reveal my name to Brajpal Singh because he would beat me up right in the classroom if he found out.

The teachers of Tyagi Inter College, Barla, thrashed the boys with kicks and fists. These kicks and fists were not those of a teacher but of a *goonda*, or hoodlum. How could a teacher beat his pupils so heartlessly?

This incident in Muzaffarnagar has remained fixed in my mind, like a question mark. This experience at the age of twelve or thirteen was painful for me. The image of that woman, whom I saw for barely a second, appears repeatedly before my eyes, along with the two wolves that kept tearing at her all night. I have often wondered if anything was left of her after the night's ordeal.

The whole college was talking about the broken rim and frame of Brajpal Singh's bicycle. Even though Bhikhuram did not reveal my name to anyone, I felt very scared the moment I set eyes on Brajpal Singh Tyagi. I found it hard to behave normally in his class. I feared that my secret was going to be exposed at any moment.

Along with science, Brajpal Singh was teaching us mathematics now. One day before the annual examination, he announced in the class, "If any student wants to ask me anything, don't hesitate. You can drop in at my house. I want every student in my class to get high marks."

One day I went to the staff room and told him that I needed help with math. He avoided me. He asked me to come to his house the next Sunday. On Sunday morning I went to his house with my book and papers. He lived on the top floor of a two-story house. His *jija*, or brother-in-law, the owner of the house, lived on the ground floor. When I got there, he and his wife were cooking something in the kitchen. As soon as he saw me, he said, "Put your books on the ledge. There is some wheat in this canister. Go get it ground. By then I will be free."

The mill was quite far. The canister was heavy, and I found it hard to carry it to the mill. But somehow I got the wheat ground. By the time I came back, he had left. When I asked his wife, she said, "I don't know where he went. He did not tell me." I sat there waiting. His wife was busy with her chores. When it got very late, she asked, "What was it you wanted from him?"

I said, "I needed to ask something about math." She got busy again. After waiting for a long time, I left. My heart was full of bitterness. He had sneaked away, sending me to get the wheat ground. Wasted my time for nothing. For several days afterward I kept feeling suffocated. No one at my house could help me.

I sat down with Sukkhan Singh and solved the math problems with his help. After this experience I resolved that I would not go chasing teachers like these. Brajpal Singh's big words were just for show. He had no hesitation in getting his private errands done. But when we needed his help, he steered clear of us or found some excuse. Somehow or other, caste got in our way. I always got poor marks in practicals—experiments or tests done in the laboratory—whereas my written exams were always graded high.

———

The exam for class ten was a board exam [for his diploma].[3] The Hindi and English exams were over. I was the first student of my caste, not just from my *basti* but from all the surrounding villages of the area, to appear for the high school exams. They were all watching me. I too had begun to realize the responsibility that I carried.

We had a one-day break before the math exam. It must have been about eight or eight-thirty in the morning. The *basti* was

———

3. Students in class ten are around sixteen years old.

quiet. Apart from the old people and the children, everyone else had left for their tasks. I was alone in my house.

Fauz Singh Tyagi, whom everyone in the village called Fauza, came and stood before me, a huge staff on his shoulder. He said, "Abey, Chuhre, what are you doing?"

"I am taking the board exams. Tomorrow I have to do the math test," I replied in a low voice.

"Study at night. Come with me. I have to sow sugarcane," Fauza ordered. I told him repeatedly that I had to study for my test the next day, but he was adamant. He held me by the elbow and dragged me to his field. He ordered me to do the work or else. My mind was set aflame by his swearing. A fire engulfed my innards that day. The memories of these crimes of the Tyagis continue to smolder deep inside me, emitting red-hot heat.

I spent the whole morning sowing cane. Like me, about eight or ten others had been brought there under duress to work for free.

Fauza's mother brought lunch. There was a tree in the field. She sat under it with the food. Many members of the Tyagi family were sitting in the shade of the tree.

Everyone was called to get his food. The unwaged sat down in the sun. No shade was left for them. They were being given two rotis and a piece of pickle in a manner that people don't use even with a beggar. I was watching all this, standing far away. I refused to take the proffered rotis. Fauza was shouting and swearing: "Abey Chuhre ke . . . Just because he has learned to read a little he has gotten above himself. Abey, don't forget who you are."

I remained standing where I was. Revolt had been born inside me. Each word of Fauza's was like a thousand stings on my body.

Finally, Fauza's mother called out, "Khajooriwali ke—come eat your rotis." Everybody called my mother Khajooriwali. Perhaps she too had forgotten her real name. In Saharanpur district, on the shores of the Hindan River, is a village named Khajoori. It is the village of my mother's family. When Fauza's mother called, I came near her. She dropped the rotis into my hand from way above, lest her hand touch mine. This gesture was insulting. I threw those rotis in front of her and ran toward my home. Fauza ran after me to beat me, but I managed to elude him.

When I told the whole story to Pitaji after I got home, he was furious. He seldom asked me to do anything by way of helping because he wanted me to be able to focus single-mindedly on my education. He constantly said that I should improve my caste by getting an education. He did not know that caste cannot be improved by education. It can be improved only by being born into the right caste.

Pitaji picked up a stick to go and fight Fauza. Ma stopped him with great difficulty.

The incident affected the entire *basti*. People had started to refuse wageless work. Something was simmering, a change was about to take place.

The Tyagis of the village turned against me. They bothered me even if I happened to pass them on the road. These were the circumstances under which I sat for the high school examination.

During exam days we encountered all sorts of problems. There was no electricity; we studied by the light of a lantern or an oil lamp. And the neighborhood was so noisy that concentrating on the books was hard, if not impossible. Fights and arguments were frequent. People would scream and provoke each other. The difference between men and women was forgotten while swearing. Even relationships were used as swear words.

Sometimes, the ear-splitting noise of drums made studying impossible. If you asked people to stop making a noise, quarrels ensued. The noise makers could not understand how their singing and playing were obstructing my studies. They would make fun of me if I complained. Pitaji tried to reason with them, but they would start advising him in return, "Why are you making a nincompoop of your son by letting him study? He will belong neither at home nor in the outside world. Educated people are generally quite foolish, anyway."

Pitaji had a different mind-set. He wanted me to get an education. He had only one thing on his mind: improving the caste.

When he got upset with me about something, he used to give the example of some Christian who had failed to study and had to resort to selling coal for a living.

Gradually, I began to socialize less and less with the people of the *basti*. I no longer found their conversation engaging. The boys of my age used to wander all day long and would frequently call on me. During the summer the boys would often go into the fields and the nearby jungle to catch rabbits. Or they would go to the pond to fish. Once I also went along and picked up two beautiful baby jackals and brought them home. Pitaji became very angry when he saw the baby jackals that I had imprisoned under a basket. It took him quite some time to calm down.

The jackals came to our house that night. Pitaji took pity on the parents and put their babies outside.

The *basti* people used to call me the quiet one, perhaps because I did not speak as much as they did. They minded my reticence. I did not participate in their day-to-day activities, either. I was absorbed in my books. In those days I was reading Premchand, Saratchandra, and Rabindranath Tagore, whose books I borrowed from the school library.

I was gradually developing a taste for literature and had also begun to try my hand at verse.

The high school results were announced in the paper. In those days they used to publish the names as well as the roll numbers. I was very happy to see my name in the paper. Pitaji invited the whole *basti* to a feast to celebrate my results. The *basti* wore a festive look that day. It was the first time that someone from our *basti* had passed high school.

Something else very special happened that day. Chamanlal Tyagi visited our home to congratulate me on my success. It was the first time a Tyagi had come to a Chuhra home to offer congratulations. Even more momentously, Chamanlal Tyagi took me to his home. Sitting close to me, he fed me lunch from their own dishes. In the all-pervasive atmosphere of untouchability, this was indeed a special gesture.

Chamanlal's oldest son was my classmate. He too had always been polite to me.

I felt very awkward during lunch. When I began to remove the dirty dishes after eating, Chamanlalji stopped me and called out to his daughter, "Come and take away Bhaiya's dishes." She came and took the dirty dishes away. His kindness made my eyes well up. I became very emotional. How could I have expected such treatment in a world where chiding and indifference were my lot? Even before this day Chamanlalji had often inquired about my studies.

I remember that I was in class three or four at the time. I could read well and could read any Hindi book at a fast pace. Chamanlal Tyagi's cowshed was close to our *basti*. One day I was passing by it. He was sitting on his porch reading the *Ramcharitmanas*.[4] He called out to me as I came near. I stopped when I heard him. "Are you Chotan ka?" he asked.

"Ji," I said.

"Come here," he said. "I hear you go to school?"

I nodded my head in affirmation.

He put the *Ramcharitmanas* in my hand. "Here, show me you can read this page." He was sitting on the cot. I took the book and started reading. He patted my back after I had read a whole page. After that day, whenever he saw me, he would inquire about my progress. He sent for Pitaji and told him, "Chotan, your son can read even the *Ramayana*." Pitaji was very pleased when he heard that. He went around, excitedly telling everyone in the *basti* about my reading prowess.

The *basti* children began to show more interest in studying after I passed high school. The *basti* began to appreciate the impor-

---

4. Classes three and four are for nine- and ten-year-old students. The *Ramcharitmanas* is the sixteenth-century Hindi version of the *Ramayana*, which was written in Sanskrit by the poet Valmiki around 300 B.C. The later version was written by Tuslidas and is popular in northern and central India.

tance of schooling a bit more, despite its economic vulnerability. I
started an evening school on our porch. Every evening I would get
fifteen or twenty children to sit in a circle for a regular class of one
to one-and-a-half hours daily. Some older people also started to
come. Many people had learned to write their name and to do a
signature. By this time my two nephews, Narendra and Devendra,
had also started going to school. Narendra was in class two and
Devendra in class one.[5] Narendra wasn't very interested in studying, but I wouldn't let him slack off. Many a time he would start
crying, but at such times I became very hard and unmoved.

———

Pitaji was going to the city, Muzaffarnagar, on some errand. I
decided to go with him. The city had a lot of roadside bookstalls.
Most of the books were of a religious nature. Pitaji stopped near
the bookstalls. He picked up one of the Gorakhpur Press books
with the distinctive red binding and put it in my hand. "What is in
the book?" he asked in a curious tone.

I said, "It is the Gita."[6] He did not know anything about the
Gita. When I told him that the book is about Lord Krishna's
advice in the *Mahabharata* to Arjun at the start of the great war, he
asked the bookseller what its price was. He was pleased to hear
that it was one rupee, fifty paise. He bought the book and gave it
to me.

When I read to him from the book after we returned home,
he was ecstatic. He was really happy. He felt that his life had been
worthwhile, that his caste had improved.

But the more I got into the book, the more my half-baked
mind was getting tied up in a quandary. I had not yet developed

———

5. These are for students of eight and seven years of age, respectively.

6. The Gita, or Bhagavad Gita (The Song of the Lord) originally was part of the epic
called the *Mahabharata*, but it became a separate book many centuries ago, perhaps the
most sacred book of the Hindus today. The Gita discusses *dharma*, or ethical conduct.

intellectually to the level where I could fully grasp the Gita's exposition on the importance of karma. What I did manage to grasp was that Krishna was inciting Arjun to go to war, that he was persuading Arjun to kill his kith and kin. That is what I thought his philosophizing about acting without desiring a reward was all about.

After every chapter in this book of knowledge was an addendum that narrated the tale of rewards that one could hope for upon reading and reflecting on that chapter. That is, the believers were being corrupted with rewards in total contradiction of the philosophy professed in the Gita. My discomfort with my reading was arousing a new consciousness in me. I began to get bored by the Gita. I wanted answers to the questions bobbing inside my head. Whenever I dared to ask my schoolteachers to answer my doubts, I got punished. They beat me up, gave me lower marks in the examinations. The taunts of my teachers and fellow students pierced me deeply. "Look at this Chuhre ka, pretending to be a Brahmin."

No one in our *basti* could answer my questions. There was no dearth of those who got drunk and went around shouting and thrashing people. In such an atmosphere searching for answers to philosophical conundrums was asking to bring down the stars from the sky.

Not only in our *basti* but also in the entire Chuhra community, as I mentioned earlier, people do not worship Hindu gods and goddesses. It is another matter for the educated among us who begin to worship them in order to assimilate. The Chuhras worship their own gods and goddesses, whose names are not to be found either in the Vedas or in the Puranas. The rituals and methods of worship are also different.

My uncle, Mausaji, the husband of my mother's sister, came to visit after a long absence. My mother wailed loudly upon his arrival.

Her sobbing proclaimed her grievance that she had not been able to see her elder sister, his wife, for so many years. Mausaji tried to calm her. "Mukundi (that was my mother's real name), why do you feel so miserable? I had family problems. Your sister has been ill . . . It is hard for us to get out."

Mausaji was an educated, religious-minded person. He dabbled in astrology. He mentioned the possibility of my becoming a writer to my mother. I didn't know then how painful it is to become a writer.

He stayed for two or three days. I presented him with that copy of the Gita when he left. He was delighted by the gift. That was my first and last meeting with Mausaji.

———

I took science in class eleven.[7] After completing high school, I gained considerable self-confidence. But circumstances began to turn against me in school. Only a couple of the other students socialized with me. Shravankumar and Chandrapal had fallen behind. Sukkhan Singh and Ram Singh were my classmates now.

Omdatta Tyagi was our English teacher. His method of speaking was satirical. He added "that is" at the end of every sentence, with a question mark. When I spoke to him about any problem, academic or personal, he would, first of all, make me aware of my being a Bhangi. On such occasions I felt that it wasn't a teacher whom I was facing but an illiterate feudal lord, drunk on his arrogance. Ram Singh was the best student of our class—and of our entire school. He might be an all-rounder, with an intellect as sharp as a blade, but he remained a Chamar, an untouchable. That was the attitude of both the teachers and the students.

One day when he and I were feeling very fed up, we wrote a character sketch of Omdatta Tyagi in English, venting our feelings.

———

7. Classes eleven and twelve (ages sixteen to eighteen) constitute the intermediate program, the completion of which is required for admission to college. In India students take two major school examinations, conducted by three examining boards, with three different syllabi. Students usually take the first examination after completing class ten, when the candidate usually is sixteen.

Its title was "A Profile of That Is." Once we had written the character sketch, when we started to read it, we were in stitches. Many other students joined us in our laughter. The whole college began to talk about the character sketch. Wherever you looked, people were quoting sentences from our sketch.

A tragedy occurred one day. It was Omdatta Tyagi's class. Ram Singh, Sukkhan Singh, and I sat at the middle desk in the front row. As soon as Omdatta stepped into the classroom, he asked Ram Singh for the English prose textbook. Ram Singh handed him the book, unaware that the character sketch that we had penned was lying inside the book. The moment Omdatta flipped the pages of the textbook, that piece of paper fell out. We all saw the paper fall. The color drained out of Ram Singh's face. Omdatta picked up the paper and started to read. His face turned livid.

He threw the book on the desk in great rage and glared at Ram Singh as though he was going to chew him up right there. The handwriting was Ram Singh's, so Omdatta's rage was completely focused on him. He ordered Ram Singh to come to the teachers' room. Ram Singh was welcomed with kicks and slaps as soon as he entered. He was ordered to adopt the rooster position and was beaten with a stick. When he got tired of assaulting Ram Singh himself, Omdatta marched him to the principal's office, where he loudly fulminated against Ram Singh. The principal let Ram Singh go with a verbal reprimand.

After this incident Omdatta used to humiliate Ram Singh whenever he found an opportunity. Ram Singh had tremendous courage. He came out laughing even after the beating he got in the teachers' room. The whole class joined him in his laughter. But I felt scared. I was mortally afraid of corporal punishment and lived in a state of permanent nervous tension.

NARENDRA KUMAR TYAGI had been recently appointed as a lecturer. He came with a master's degree in mathematics. He had an innocent look, a soft voice, and extremely polite manners. Narendra Kumar taught math to classes eleven and twelve.

It was March or April 1965.[1] Narendra Kumar Tyagi was in the classroom. The summer's heat had made him thirsty. I was sitting in the seat right in front of him. He said to me, "Go, bring me a glass of water from the pitcher." Two huge pitchers, full of cold water, were kept in front of the principal's office. The moment Narendra Tyagi asked me to get him water, the classroom buzzed with whispers. I got up to go but then came back. I said to him, "Master Sahib, I am not permitted even to touch those pitchers. Please send someone else."

Master Sahib was surprised. He asked, "Why?"

I replied quietly, "I belong to the Chuhra caste."

The look on his face registered his shock. He stared unblinkingly at me. I said, "If you still want me to get you water, I will go."

He came out of his trance. "No . . . sit down." And he went to get the water himself.

I felt that even though this man had a master's degree in mathematics, he was a coward. He didn't have the courage to drink water from my hand. I began thinking of Chandrapal and Shravankumar. They weren't very bright in their studies, but they were wonderful human beings. They were my beloved friends who were unafraid of "losing caste" [becoming polluted by associating with someone from a lower caste].

---

1. The author was then nearly fifteen.

These assaults of untouchability have ripped me apart time and time again.

———

Brajpal Singh was still teaching chemistry. I had not an iota of respect for him in my heart. I had never, however, exhibited any disrespect toward him publicly. I enjoyed studying chemistry. My marks in chemistry in class eleven's annual exams were very good. But soon after starting class twelve, I felt that whenever I went to the lab for practicals or experiments that would be counted in the examinations, Brajpal would keep me out on some pretext or other.

This was my last year in the intermediate program, and I would take a board examination at the end of term. My whole future depended on how well I did on this examination. When I was unable to do any lab experiments after trying for several months, I began to feel certain that I was being kept out deliberately. I asked him, "What have I done? Have I damaged anything?" But Brajpal didn't bother to reply.

When I told Ram Singh of my problem, he suggested that I go and meet the principal. The principal, Yashveer Tyagi, heard me attentively. He assured me that he wouldn't let anything happen to me. He said he would talk to Brajpal Singh to solve the problem. But what happened was just the opposite. I was unable to conduct any experiments during that whole year. Not only did I do very poorly in the lab tests on the board exam but I also got low marks on the oral, even though I answered the examiner's questions quite correctly.

When the results were announced, I was among the failures. I had good marks in all other subjects except chemistry. I had failed the lab tests.

This turn of events put a horrendous barrier in my path. I no longer felt interested in studying. I couldn't make up my mind about what to do next. I felt surrounded by darkness. My family seemed to be in mourning. Pitaji became very quiet after telling me

how sorry he was. I felt very down, unable to put my mind to anything. That was a terrible time for me.

Around this time Maya's wedding took place. Making the
arrangements for the marriage helped me forget my own worries
for a short while. The uncertain future stood ready to devour me.
While I was trying so hard to break out of the confined world of
the Chuhres, my circumstances kept pushing me back in. Brajpal's
conspiracy had broken me apart.

My older brother Jasbir was working at the Survey of India in
Dehra Dun. He was staying with our mother's brother, whom we
called Mama. When I recounted my sad tale to Jasbir, he said,
"Come on, let this village go to hell. Come to Dehra Dun and
study there. I will get you admitted to DAV College.[2] Why are you
worrying? You will definitely pass next year."

I had found a foothold, and my foundering hopes revived.
Jasbir gave me a pep talk in his very distinctive style: "Come on.
This is nothing. Why do you worry so much when I am here?"
However massive the problem, Jasbir could wrestle it down in a
minute with this pet statement of his. He never felt hopeless.

Pitaji gave me permission to go to Dehra Dun. The day I left
home, he became very emotional, telling me, "Son, you are a child
of a poor Chuhra. Always remember that."

I left for Dehra Dun with Surjan, immediately after Maya's
vida, her departure to her husband's home. My wardrobe consist-
ed of an old shirt and a pair of pajamas made of long-cloth. Pitaji
hadn't given me a single extra paisa over the bus fare. How could
he, anyway? He had taken a loan for Maya's wedding, and Jasbir's
entire salary went to pay it off. The family was living hand to

---

2. Dayanand Anglo-Vedic College, one of many founded by the Arya Samaj, a right-
wing Hindu reform movement that was begun by Dayanand Saraswati (1824–83).
Most popular in northern India, it urged the abandonment of rituals and idol worship in favor of a return to the Vedas, proclaiming it to be a "purer" form of
Hinduism. It also aimed to educate and modernize Hindus. Because the education
was along Western lines and supposedly in conformity to the Vedas, the colleges were
called "Anglo-Vedic." See also the introduction.

mouth. Getting on the bus to Dehra Dun, my heart was sad. It felt as though Barla was receding behind me forever. Yet the bleak memories of Barla have left a permanent impression on me. Their bitter taste is still lurking in some corner of my mind and comes to the fore at the slightest provocation.

Uncle lived in Indresh Nagar. Alongside Khadri Mohalla, near Saharanpur Chowk, is an open sewer. Indresh Nagar is across this open sewer. This densely populated area was originally known as Jatia Mohalla. Later on its name was changed to Indresh Nagar. Uncle and Jasbir lived in one room. Surjan lived with his in-laws. He would come without fail to see his father, that is, our uncle, for a few minutes during the afternoon and for an extended visit in the evening. I was the third person in the room that Mama and Jasbir shared. The room was practically bare. A string went across the room on which dirty clothes were piled in a disorderly manner. The room, littered with their stuff, looked unkempt. A clean-up happened only rarely.

My brother Janesar lived nearby. His room was made of planks of wood. The roof was covered by an old piece of tin. The room was as messy as ours. A stove occupied one corner of the room, and the whole interior, including the clothes, had turned black from the smoke. Bimla Bhabhi, my sister-in-law, had now been in Dehra Dun for a year. She had also picked up work in some homes. She left home in the morning and came back in the afternoon. Janesar did not have a regular job. He worked at whatever came his way. Often he worked on the night shift for the municipal garbage truck.

Surjan Singh had gained admission to grade eleven at the DAV College, but I had not managed to get accepted yet. The seal of "Inter-fail" had been stamped on my forehead. The moment people found out, they would raise their eyebrows. After much running around I managed to get admitted with the help of Premkumar Sharmaji's recommendation. Surjan Singh had begged him with great persistence. Sharmaji was a well-known teacher at DAV College. His face would acquire a disapproving look the moment my certificate from Inter College, Barla, was thrust in front of him.

Running around for my admission, I went through bouts of total hopelessness. Many a time I felt that I wouldn't be able to complete my education. My self-confidence had been badly shaken by my failure. I felt that life had nothing left for me.

Surjan Singh's wife, Swarnlata, lived in her parental home. I visited Surjan and Swarnlata often. She was very affectionate and treated me like her kin. She shored me up in my moments of despair.

I plunged into my studies the moment I got admitted. DAV College was quite far from Indresh Nagar, but despite that I never missed the 7 A.M. class. I wanted to get rid of my feelings of futility. Gradually, I was beginning to get out of my dark cave of wretchedness.

Indresh Nagar was settled mostly by the untouchable castes of Bhangis, who worked as sweepers or cleaners, and Jatias, who made and repaired shoes. Bhangis now liked to call themselves Valmikis, and Jatias preferred to be called Jatavs. The two castes lived in separate areas, the Valmikis on one side and the Jatavs on the other. The entrance to the Valmikis' neighborhood was from Saharanpur Road and to the Jatavs' from Kanvli Road. Poverty and illiteracy were the ancestral legacy of both. They all lived a constricted, deprived life in little cubbyholes. Only a few got to eat two proper meals a day.

The sweepers left home at five in the morning. The clanging sound of the iron carts that they used to collect the garbage woke everyone up. Both women and men went to work early in the morning. Only the elderly, the sick, and the children stayed behind. The schoolchildren loitered in the streets all day. Few children took an interest in their studies. How could the parents find

the time to take them by hand and drop them off at school?
Leaving home at five, the parents would return around twelve or
one. After washing up, the women went to the homes that they
worked in to pick up rotis. They would have to go back to work
around two, and it would be five by the time they returned. They
had neither the time nor the desire to know what their children
did all day or whether they went to school.

I went to college on foot. As I had mentioned earlier, the college was quite far from Indresh Nagar. Jasbir bought me a bicycle
after a couple of months, paying for it a little bit at a time. I was
able to save a lot of time in commuting after I got the bicycle. The
first period began at seven in the morning. The math teacher was
very punctual. Hardly fifteen to twenty students of the sixty or
seventy enrolled attended the morning class. I never skipped this
class. The atmosphere here was quite different from Tyagi Inter
College. I did not have proper clothes to wear to college. In the village it didn't matter if one wore a dirty, unironed shirt and long-
cloth pajamas. Here everybody wore trousers and shirts. Jasbir
gave me one of his old pairs of trousers, which was quite loose on
me. It served as my collegewear. Many boys in the class would
make fun of my country looks. Because I was new in college and
unfamiliar with its ways, I kept quiet, although I was quite used to
taunts and neglect. I feel amazed when I look back on those days
and the things that I learned to tolerate. How much my ability to
tolerate hurts flung at me has taken out of me!

One day, just as I was coming out of the English class, a boy
from another section waylaid me. He had three or four other boys
with him. They began to make fun of me. One began to pull down
my trousers, "Which tailor did you go to? Give us his address too."
The other boys were laughing loudly. I wanted to get away from
them, but they would not let me go. Some were pulling at my
trousers and others at my shirt. I entreated piteously, "It will tear
. . . please let go." They laughed heartily at my rural accent. One of
them asked, "Which village has your majesty arrived from?" Their
mockery stung me deeply.

This drama went on for a long time. Trapped among them, I was helpless. I wonder how long they would have tormented me, if a senior teacher hadn't happened to come by, making them run away. The teacher asked my name and the class I was in, and I replied, "Ji . . . Omprakash Valmiki, class twelve, section J."

I went to my next class, but I couldn't concentrate. I couldn't follow the lecture. Somehow or the other the period came to an end. I started looking for Surjan as soon as I got out. He was sitting in his class, and I gestured to him to come out. As soon as he did so, I told him what had happened. A boy named Bahadur Singh Thapa was in his class. He was from Rajpur. Surjan asked him to come out too and recounted the whole story to him. Bahadur asked me, "Will you be able to recognize that boy? Which class is he in?"

The three of us went and stood in front of his class. That boy was sitting in the back row with his friends.

Bahadur said to me, "You go. I will fix him right now. He will never bother you again."

I left them and stood at a distance. Surjan and Bahadur stayed near the classroom. As soon as the class was over, the boy came out with his friends. Bahadur motioned to him to come close and the moment he did so, Bahadur handed him two or three slaps. The sudden attack unsettled the boy. He began to whimper, "Dauji . . . Why are you hitting me? What have I done?"

Bahadur pulled at his collar. "Tell me, who tailors your clothes? Shall I send you to him naked? Or shall I get him here? Next time you ask someone for his tailor's address—"

The boy begged for forgiveness with folded hands, "Dauji . . . Please forgive me . . . I made a mistake."

Gradually, I began to adjust to the new environment. I also made some friends. I was no longer alone. My rural background no longer made me feel weak or submissive. All of Surjan's friends

now recognized me. Most of them were the aggressive, macho
types, and I didn't much care for them. Still, I needed to socialize
with them. I began to make friends in my class as well. A boy
named Purushottam had become a good friend. Several other
companions also helped me adjust to life in the city. Many people
in Indresh Nagar were going to college. Bhukanlal was getting his
master's. Hemlal was in class twelve at Hindu National. There
was Gopi and several others. We met almost every day. We made
all sorts of plans. We were all greatly enthusiastic about doing
social work.

Although Indresh Nagar seemed to be close-knit to outsiders,
internally it was divided in two. The relations between the
Valmikis and the Jatavs were tense. They would often get into
brawls and beat each other up. Two or three families called Bhatde
lived in Indresh Nagar as well. Bhatdes, who are Sikhs, fought
among themselves daily. Sometimes they would draw swords. At
such times their women would drag the men inside. There would
be a huge uproar.

Hemlal was a Jatav, and our friendship had deepened into
intimacy. We also visited each other's homes, which was quite a
risky thing to do during those days. Uncle cautioned me several
times. He was upset that I was befriending a Jatav when the same
Jatavs had come right up to our house to beat up Surjan. Despite
all these obstacles, Hemlal and I continued to meet. Whenever I
visited his home, his mother, sisters, and sister-in-law all treated
me with a great deal of affection. His baby sister was very cute
and doll-like.

Indresh Nagar had a library run by the Jatavs that had been
started by a grant from the government. The library had a huge
supply of Gandhiana, and I read several books by Gandhi in this
library. One day when I was siting in the library, looking at some
books, Hemlal put a small book in my hand. As I was flipping its
pages, Hemlal said, "You must read this book." The name of the
book was *Dr. Ambedkar: A Biography*. Its author was Chandrika
Prasad Jigyasu.

Ambedkar was an unknown entity to me then. I knew about Gandhi, Nehru, Vallabhbhai Patel, Rajendra Prasad, Radhakrishnan, Vivekananda, Tagore, Saratchandra, Bhagat Singh, Subhas Bose, Chandrashekhar Azad, Savarkar, and so on but was completely ignorant about Ambedkar. Despite my twelve years of studying at Tyagi Inter College, Barla, I had never encountered this name. The college library also did not have a single book on Ambedkar. I had never heard this name from a teacher's or a scholar's mouth. On Republic Day we heard countless narratives of devotion to the country, but they never included the name of the author of the Constitution. All the media of communication had been unable to inform people like me about this name.

I asked Hemlal, "Who is this Ambedkar?" A sliver of a smile parted his lips. "We'll talk after you have finished reading the book."

I came home with the book. There was nothing special in the opening pages. But the further I went into the book, I felt as though a new chapter about life was being unfurled before me. A chapter about which I had known nothing. Ambedkar's lifelong struggle shook me up. I spent many days and nights in great turmoil. The restlessness inside increased. My stonelike silence suddenly began to melt. I proceeded to read all of Ambedkar's books that I found in the library.

I expressed my gratitude to Hemlal. He had truly shown me a new path. Reading these books had awakened my consciousness. These books had given voice to my muteness. During this period an antiestablishment consciousness became strong in me.

From textbooks to the media of communication, they were all beating the drum about Gandhi. I had heard many *savarnas*, upper-caste people, abuse Gandhi in day-to-day conversations—that this old man had turned the heads of the Bhangis and the Chamars by naming them and all untouchables Harijans, the children of God. How wrong was their anger about Gandhi. After reading Ambedkar, I realized that by naming the untouchables Harijans, Gandhi had not helped them to join the national mainstream but had saved the Hindus from becoming a minority.

Guarded their interests, in fact. Yet these upper castes were angry
with him because he had turned Harijans' heads! The Poona
Pact episode completely erased any illusions that I had harbored
about Gandhi.[3] The Poona Pact was what had made Ambedkar
lose heart.

A new word, *Dalit*, entered my vocabulary, a word that is not
a substitute for *Harijan* but an expression of the rage of millions of
untouchables. A new direction was opening for me. I was also
beginning to realize that the education imparted in schools and
colleges did not make us secular but turned us into narrow-mind-
ed, fundamentalist Hindus. The deeper I was getting into this literature, the more articulate my rage became. I began to debate
with my college friends and put my doubts before my teachers.
This literature gave me courage.

I became more active in college events. In Dehra Dun
protests against using English instead of Hindi were in full swing.
The students of DAV College were in the forefront of these
protests. All the billboards and signboards in English were paint-
ed over with black paint. I was participating in these activities and
would get home late. My uncle would scold me every day. The
more active I became, the more opposition I faced at home. In the
village Pitaji had never interfered in my life. But here I was being
reprimanded daily.

A huge procession marched from DAV College. The police
stopped it before the clock tower, near the bus terminal. Tension
in the city was great. The situation deteriorated to such an extent
that the police fired on the supporters of Hindi. One student died.
Many were injured. The passion of the students dissipated after
this tragedy.

My uncle ordered me not to leave home that day. Yet I did. I

---

3. In 1931 Gandhi went on a hunger strike until Ambedkar withdrew his support for
separate representation of untouchables, which Gandhi believed would be a very
divisive force in Hindu society. Ambedkar capitulated because the Mahatma was
extremely weak and frail, and the entire nation wondered whether he would survive
the ordeal. See also the introduction.

had to listen to his lecture for hours after I returned. "What would I tell my sister and brother-in-law if something happened to you?" He delivered this diatribe every two minutes. He would also make vulgar comments about my friends in his sermon. Jasbir became totally quiet when Uncle got on his high horse. Janesar remained totally uninvolved in these disputes. When I said anything to Jasbir, he had only one thing to say: "You have come here to study. Stop getting involved in these useless things." I felt that my involvement in these protests was an essential part of my education. But for Uncle and Jasbir it was a waste of time.

We got into a big argument one day. I had been with Hemlal all day. He and I had talked about nothing but our studies that day. Uncle's lecture started the moment I returned home. I tried to acquaint him with my side of things, but he kept screaming at me and making abusive comments about my friends. I exploded. "Uncle, all my friends are studious. I do not go around with bullies or hooligans. I do nothing else besides studying."

I don't know which of his weak spots I touched that day. He was infuriated and threatened to send me back to the village.

I feared that once again my education would be interrupted. I was determined to continue with my studies, whatever the cost. So I decided to compromise. But Uncle continued to find occasions to scold me. There was a great deal of tension between us. Because we lived in one room, eating and sleeping together, I would try very hard not to upset him. I failed to placate him, however, even though I tended his hookah and massaged his legs and his head. My relationship with my cousin Surjan also suffered. He always sided with his father. Sometimes he magnified and reported my smallest infractions to Uncle, and as a result, his father's anger would rain down on me in the form of a long lecture.

I was living under a great deal of stress. I became very irritable. I no longer went to Surjan's in-laws' place. Hemlal was the only person I could talk to.

Premchand, an Indresh Nagar friend, once was a student leader. He had left his studies and gone to live in Roorkee, where he ran some sort of union. He had filled out a nomination form for the Roorkee seat in the 1967 provincial elections. Eight or ten Indresh Nagar boys had gone to Roorkee to work in his election campaign. Hemlal and I also went. I did not ask my uncle's permission. My brother Jasbir too had only been informed. When I was leaving for Roorkee, Uncle said to Jasbir, "Tell him not to come back here. He will have to go back to the village." I kept quiet. Bhukanlal, Sianand, Hemlal, and the others were waiting for me outside. I left with them without saying a word.

I sent a letter to Pitaji as soon as I got to Roorkee, through the bus driver on the Roorkee-Barla bus, who delivered it at Buddhu's tea stall at the Barla bus station. Buddhu took it to Pitaji. Pitaji came to Roorkee the very next day, and I told him everything. He listened to me quietly. I felt frightened inside. What if he also didn't like my coming to Roorkee for the election campaign? But all he said was, "You do whatever you think is right. I am an illiterate boor. Just don't bring shame on me. As far as your education is concerned, you are going back straight to Dehra Dun afterward. Tell Harphool [Uncle] that I gave him shelter at Barla when he knew nothing. After him, I put up his lad for two years. He has forgotten all that. If he doesn't want to keep you, I will make some other arrangement for you. Why do you worry?"

Pitaji left for Dehra Dun immediately after that. I knew what was going to happen there. My uncle would offer him liquor. Pitaji would fight with him after downing a few drinks. Both would be at each other's throat.

We walked around Roorkee's neighborhoods and nearby villages, campaigning for our friend. The canvassing provided me with the opportunity to see the lives of people at close range. I heard their stories of deprivation. Most people did not understand the true meaning of democracy or the value of one's vote. They couldn't grasp the importance of stuffing a piece of paper in the ballot box. How innocent were those people, totally uncomprehending of the meaning or value of independence. But, then, had independence truly reached them? The pimps of the rulers were exploiting them for their own ends.

My brother Janesar told me about the row between Pitaji and Uncle on my return to Dehra Dun. My uncle's bitterness toward me was even greater after Pitaji's visit. He felt that I had incited Pitaji. For his part, Pitaji had said a lot of things that Uncle had found hard to digest.

I went back to my studies. My pockets were empty. I left for college early in the morning on an empty stomach. I would light a fire in the stove and scramble something together on my return from college in the afternoon. My brother Jasbir dropped by sometimes. Bimla Bhabhi, my sister-in-law, had gone to visit her parents. Uncle would return in the afternoon with rotis from the homes that he serviced. But I never felt like eating them. I would lose my appetite by just looking at them.

We were surviving somehow or other. In the evening Janesar and I would go to the wood depot where we would get some money for loading and unloading the wood. We would net five to ten rupees after working for a couple of hours, enough for our pocket money. Off-loading trucks was tiring work. Janesar was used to it, but I found it very hard. When I had a few rupees in my pocket, I would go to Maheshwar's tea stall during my free period and snack on tea and rolls. Both items cost only fifty paise. My stomach remained empty when my money ran out.

I also tutored children for a while. We had started an evening school in Indresh Nagar. Bhukanlal was the one who had planned it. The school closed as soon as Bhukanlal got a job at IRDE (Instrument Research and Development Establishment). Jasbir worked for the Survey of India. Half his salary went to pay off the family's loans. The interest rate on the loan we had taken for Maya's wedding was exorbitant, and very little money was left after paying the moneylender.

The first winter in Dehra Dun was extremely difficult for me. I had no woolen clothes. One could manage by wrapping oneself with a bedsheet or a blanket in a village school's classroom, but that wasn't an option at the city college. I needed a sweater badly.

The Dehra Dun municipality gave a khaki jersey to the sanitation employees. They also got a dark-colored thick *khaddar,* or handloom shirt. This uniform identified the sanitation workers. The *jamadars,* or sweepers, could thus be spotted from a distance.

I managed to save thirty or forty rupees by working at the wood depot. I bought a khaki jersey from a municipal employee with those rupees. Although I had it dyed green at the dry cleaner's, you could still tell it was a municipal jersey.

The first day I wore it to college, the boys began to tease me by calling me a sweeper. Although the sweater did protect me from the winter cold, the taunts of the boys were even more piercing than the cold. Many a time I determined not to wear it. But finally, I made up my mind. I decided to see how long they would go on taunting me.

I still had some money left after buying the jersey. I bought some thick wool from the Tibetan market at a very cheap rate. Swarnlata Bhabhi, my cousin Surjan's wife, knitted a short-sleeved sweater for me with this wool. The jersey and the sweater saved me during my first Dehra Dun winter.

One day in college some boys were talking about a training course. Purushottam was among them. I too had gone and sat down with them, but I could not follow what they were talking about. When I asked Purushottam to explain after they had left, he said, "There is a bomb factory in Raipur where they train you to operate the machines. They take boys with a high school diploma."

I said to him. "Let's go to Raipur and find out."

He asked, "Do you know where this factory is?"

"Yes, I have been to Raipur a couple of times with Surjan," I replied.

Purushottam and I went off to Raipur. When we asked the security guard at the main entrance of IRDE, he told us that the ordnance factory was farther down. We inquired again at the main gate of the ordnance factory and were asked to wait. After about

JOOTHAN   89

ten minutes a man came to the door and asked, "Who was inquiring about the training?"

I said, "I was."

The man said, "The next batch will be admitted in July. You two should send a letter to the general manager. A form will be mailed to your home address."

We went to the Raipur ordnance factory's post office right away, bought postcards to write to the general manager, and put them in a letterbox then and there.

I received a form at my home address after a fortnight or so. I filled it out and sent it back without telling anybody. They called me for a written examination after a few days. I passed the written exam and was called for the oral, which I also cleared.

I abandoned my college education when I got the apprenticeship at the ordnance factory in Dehra Dun.[4] I knew absolutely nothing about the work before my induction into the factory. All I knew was that I did not want to go into the line of work that my ancestors had been doing for thousands of years.

I wrote to Pitaji, informing him of my decision to leave college and learn this technical work in a government factory. He was delighted. He kept saying repeatedly, "At last you have escaped 'caste.'" But what he didn't know till the day he died is that caste follows one right up to one's death.

I had begun to dream of self-reliance. I found it hard to forget the days of my life that I lived in extreme poverty. The technical education promised to make it possible for me to earn two meals a day. I began to receive a monthly stipend of 107 rupees a month during my apprenticeship, which seemed like a princely sum to me. As soon as I received the money, I would put the entire amount in Jasbir's hand. He would give me back twenty rupees for pocket money.

I left home at 7 A.M., returning at 5:30 in the evening. I went on my bike. Jasbir used to put two or three *paranthas* [fried flat

4. Raipur is a neighborhood that houses many public institutions; now a part of Dehra Dun.

bread) in my bag, which I ate at lunchtime. After making the *paranthas* for me, Jasbir would leave with our uncle to help him in his work. Uncle was posted in front of the train station on Gandhi Road. Besides the hotels, the area also had a tonga, or a horse-drawn carriage, stand. The hotels and the tonga stand helped Uncle make a little extra money on the side. Jasbir would go on to his office afterward.

That was the daily routine. Liquor was the binding force between Uncle and Jasbir. They drank together in the evening. This addiction proved fatal for Jasbir. It was the cause of his untimely death.

One day on my way to the factory, I bumped into Kamla near the Darshanlal intersection. Kamla was Girvar's daughter, and she was in training at ITI (Industrial Training Institute). We were Girvar's tenants. Kamla waved me to stop. She was running late. Because ITI was on the way to the ordnance factory, she sat behind me on the carrier [bicycle]. I dropped her off at Survey Chowk.

When I came home that evening, Uncle was ready to do bat-tle. I don't know if Uncle had seen us himself or someone had informed him. Kamla's taking a lift from me was a great crime in his eyes. Jasbir scolded me endlessly. I tried to reason with them that it was a mere coincidence, but they were unwilling to listen. Together they created such a ruckus that I fell totally quiet. Their allegations against me were totally groundless. They were imput-ing and inferring things that had not entered my mind. A small incident had been blown out of proportion. I felt awful. I wanted to run away.

That night was full of torment for me. Girvar's family and ours shared the same courtyard. We were together night and day. Even if I had given Kamla a lift on my bike, was it such a big crime that they had to humiliate me to such an extent? I had begun to feel restless. I was looking for a way that would let me escape this life.

Books were my greatest friends. They kept up my morale. I
started tutoring in the evening at a couple of homes after returning from the factory. I would keep myself busy so as not to get in
Uncle's way. I read a lot of fiction during these days, translations
from English and Bengali. Ambedkar's books were nowhere to be
found, even if you searched hard.

—

It was the Dussehra vacation.[5] There was a circuit house in the
cantonment, and Phool Singh was the cook there.[6] Surjan visited
him often. He knew Phool Singh through his in-laws, and there
was some sort of a family connection as well. We went there early
in the morning on the day of Dussehra. A lot of activities of the
cantonment took place in a huge open field, or *maidan*, near the
circuit house. The field even had a helipad. Whenever a VIP came
to Dehra Dun, his helicopter landed on this strip.

This large open space would see a lot of hustle and bustle on
Dussehra day. Surjan and I also went to see the festivities.
Thousands of people were gathered. The crowd was gathered
around a small pit where a huge buffalo was tied to a post in a corner. Near it stood a small army battalion. A tent was pitched on
one side, where the invited guests and their families sat on chairs.
A band was playing in another corner, and some people were trying to dance to the tune. The whole atmosphere was suffused with
excitement and festiveness.

A muscular man entered the field, pushing his way through
the crowd. The only garment on his body was red underpants. A
turban covered his head, he wore a garland of marigolds around
his neck. His forehead sported a red mark. He seemed like a
wrestler. Carrying a huge *khukri*, a curved knife, in his hand, he

---

5. Dussehra is the tenth day of the mother goddess Durga's festival.

6. The circuit house, a legacy of the British Empire, is a government-owned guest
house.

came and stood near the buffalo. Behind him walked a Brahmin priest with a steel platter full of the materials needed for the religious ceremony. The priest threw vermilion, rice, and turmeric on the buffalo; he smeared his horns with turmeric, reciting some Sanskrit verses in a loud voice as he did all that.

As soon as the ceremony ended, an army officer ordered the soldiers to attention. Then he commanded them to fire in the air. Simultaneously, the wrestler-like man picked up the curved knife and brought it down on the buffalo's neck. The head and torso of the buffalo separated within the batting of an eyelid. Blood squirted like a fountain from the buffalo's neck and collected in the pit. A great wave of excitement spread through the crowd as soon as the buffalo's neck was cut. People began to dance, shout, and scream. Cocks and rams were being butchered in another part of the field. I found the atmosphere frightful, a festival of murders.

I asked Surjan if we could leave. I was feeling stifled and found it difficult to keep standing. The sacrificing of animals in the name of the *shakti puja*, the offering made to the mother goddess Durga, disturbed me greatly. The buffalo's head hanging from the post was hovering in front of my eyes. Its headless body lay at a short distance.

Animal sacrifice in Dehra Dun and the surrounding areas was quite common. In Garhwal buffaloes were annually sacrificed at the temple of Kheravadni Devi. This temple is at a place called Kanda in the Pauri District. Buffaloes are sacrificed at this temple on the day after Diwali [a religious holiday]. The Kalinka Fair, which is organized under the auspices of the development officers of Borokhal (Garhwal) and Malda (Almora-Kumaon), near the Garhwal-Kumaon boundary, has been the site of twenty-five hundred to three thousand animal sacrifices. The district administrators, MLAs (elected members of the Legislative Assembly), and the political party leaders are present at these traditional fairs, which are held in the name of religious rituals and the fulfillment of vows. The sacrifices of buffaloes and sheep are carried out in their presence. Liquor is sold freely at the fair. The famous five-hundred-year-old Kalinka Fair, as important as the famous Nauchandi Fair of Meerut and the Kamakshi Fair of Tamil Nadu, is held every three years. Volunteers of the Pradeshik Seva Dal [a social work organization], Home Guards, and the employees of the revenue service maintain law and order at this huge fair.

The ancient Kalinka Fair is regarded as an exquisite example of the cultural unity of Garhwal-Kumaon. Women come to the fair adorned in traditional costumes and jewelry. Men dance to folk tunes, axes in hand. The fair is a mirror of this region's culture and civilization, one more link in the animal sacrifice fairs of Kanda, Mundaneshwar, Bunkhal, and so on. In the light of contemporary perspectives on animal sacrifice, how do such rituals supposedly promote religious exaltation? That the same thing should happen in Uttarakhand (the mountains near Dehra Dun) is an outrage because this area is where the gods and goddesses are popularly thought to reside, and such bloodletting would be anathema to them. For me, animal sacrifice is a symbol of a terribly inhumane and violent mind-set.

———

After a year's training at the ordnance factory, I took a competitive examination and was selected. I was to go to Jabalpur for further training. I would spend two years at the Ordnance Factory Training Institute in Khamaria [Khamaria is a section of the city of Jabalpur]. This selection opened new doors for my career and my life changed for the better.

I went back to the village to see Pitaji and Ma before leaving for Jabalpur. Pitaji was pleased. He said, "The farther you go, the more you will get to see the world." But Ma became anxious. She had never even heard of Jabalpur. She kept asking, "How many *kos* is Jabalpur from here?"[7] Ma hadn't seen Delhi either, although she had heard of it. Ma was concerned about where was I going to live,

———

7. A *kos* is an old measure of distance, about two miles; used seldom today.

what I would eat. What sort of language did the people of Jabalpur speak? and so on. When I told her that I was going to live in the hostel and eat in the mess, that too at government expense, she felt a bit reassured. She tied two or three kilos of solid molasses in a piece of cloth for me.

Pitaji offered me a lot of encouragement. Jabalpur was a foreign country for all my family members.

After my return to Dehra Dun, I started my preparations for Jabalpur. Viyaj Bahadur Soul, who came from Hoshiarpur, Punjab, was also going to Jabalpur with me. He came from a farming family in Kabirpur village in Haryana. He was a Punjabi Jat.[8] We had become great friends during our training. He spoke mostly in Punjabi. He stumbled often when he tried to speak Hindi.

When we got to the train station to travel to Jabalpur, it was crowded with boys from the training institute. In this crowd were Jasbir, Janesar, Bimla, Surjan, Rahti Bhabhi, who had come from the village for a couple of days, Swarnlata Bhabhi, and her younger sister Chandrakala, whom everyone called Chanda. They had all come to bid farewell to me. These moments of parting were heavy. Among all our deprivations some delicate tendrils linked us.

Our train left for a new and unfamiliar world. We left behind all the familiar faces. What remained with us were a few memories.

As the train gathered speed, the sadness of parting began to lift. Kulbhushan Nayyar started his usual bantering. He too had been selected for further training in Jabalpur.

We got off at Jabalpur station on the evening of July 1, 1968, between 5 and 6 P.M. The students of the Ordnance Factory Training Institute met our train. We breathed a sigh of relief on seeing them. The senior students welcomed us with open arms and brought us to the residence. The allotment of rooms was pre-arranged. I was placed in room number 3, hostel number 1.

---

8. Jat is a middle-ranking caste, traditionally of agriculturalists and military personnel. Jats now are working in many professions, and they wield considerable political and economic power.

I was introduced to a new world after entering the training institute's residence. I found a lot of things new and strange. I didn't have to worry about my board and lodging. The hostel was home to about two hundred students. It was a lively place. The residence's evenings brimmed with excitement. Just as a thicket begins to resound with the chirping of birds at sunset, the hostel came alive with singing, music, sports, laughter, spirited conversation, and many other activities after sundown.

The hostel was situated in a quiet area. On one side was the ordnance factory in Khamaria; on the other were the garrison engineer's office, the institute's main building, the auditorium, and the main road. The residential areas were quite a distance from the hostel. There was a big *nala*, a wastewater canal, behind the hostel that separated it from the city.

The training institute had a set daily routine. We had to leave for the institute's workshop at 7:30 A.M. The workshop was inside the ordnance factory. Tea and breakfast were served at seven in the morning. Lunch was at twelve. After lunch we had classes in technical education from 1 to 4:30 P.M. in the main building of the institute. Here we studied engineering and related subjects.

The student-run mess committee looked after the mess. Even though it was based on mutual cooperation, fights often erupted on account of the food. The arbitrary use of power by senior students came to the fore on such occasions. The students often complained about the partially cooked rotis. Sometimes they even resorted to blows. Vijay Bahadur and I had a totally different perspective from the others vis-à-vis the rawness of rotis. I never complained about them. When Vijay Bahadur saw someone throwing away the rotis, he would get furious. "You ass! You don't know the value of this roti! How much labor has been put in the field to grow it—do you know?" No one dared throw the rotis when he began his oratory.

Really, who else but a farmer can know the cost of roti? Since I was a child, I have considered roti an immensely valuable thing. Those who wasted it seemed criminal to me.

The days in residence at the factory were days of fun for some. For me, these were the days of finding myself.

I came across the game of chess for the first time after I began to live in the residence. This game of elephants and horses attracted me, and I learned it pretty fast. Many of my companions in the residence sat down to play chess the moment they returned from the institute. I had a teacher named O. P. Garg, who was very fond of chess. When he found out that I loved it too, he began to frequent the hostel to play with me. Many a time we would play late into the night. During those days I was so intoxicated with chess that my brain would be constantly preoccupied with thinking about the moves.

Around this time I read Premchand's short story, "The Chess Players." The story made me feel that chess could become such a fatal addiction that one could forget one's home, one's family, one's country. Oh, what a story! After reading it, I felt agitated for days. It affected me to such an extent that I began to avoid the game. The addiction to chess had not lasted long. That I had missed being an expert chess player by a hair's breadth didn't bother me at all. In fact, I was happy to have the self-control to give it up.

The new surroundings and the new environment gave me new experiences. The hostel was huge, large enough to accommodate as many as five hundred students. The rooms were very large, and ten to twelve students shared a room. The students came from different parts of the country. The ones in my room were from Dehra Dun, Muradnagar, Kanpur, and Poona.

All had their own bedding except me. On arrival everyone was provided with an iron-frame bed and a steel chair. The built-in closet substituted for the desk. I faced the problem of bedding the moment I arrived at the residence. I had a cheap suitcase that contained a few clothes. I had also brought some books and papers. Vijay Bahadur and I slept in the same bed for several days. After about a month I bought the cloth from a shopkeeper in Ranjhi and got a mattress made on credit. I paid it off in small monthly installments. After deducting the mess dues, I had little money left out of my monthly stipend to pay for my day-to-day expenses. I barely managed to keep afloat. I was not in a position to live a life of fun and games like some of my fellow students. I tried to save some money out of my stipend every month so that I could send a money order to Pitaji.

Some students had Marxist leanings, and I started to read Marxist literature after coming into contact with them. Gorky's *Mother*, especially, shook me up. I also became acquainted with Chekhov's short stories. I joined these Marxists in forming a theater group. We rehearsed in the hostel. We staged many plays in the institute's auditorium.

I began to write poetry. A student named Govind Maurya next door was always lost in his books. Rahi Masoom Raza's *Adha Ganv* got a lot of attention from the critics, and Govind Maurya made me read it. Yashpal's *Jhootha Sach* kept me awake for many nights.

The day I entered the hostel, I found a copy of Rajendra Yadav's *Sara Aakash* in the desk drawer. I stayed in that room for two years and read this novel several times. I have not seen a better book on middle-class life. Many other students also borrowed the novel and read it.

I also began to write short one-act plays and to stage them. I did both acting and directing. It was the beginning of my involvement in theater. Shri Vermaji was a well-known theater person in Khamaria. I staged several plays under his direction. We also put up a shadow play for the Gandhi centenary in the big *maidan*, or public park, of Khamaria.

Vijay Bahadur Soul and I lived in the same hostel. Both of us knew the anguish of having our education interrupted, and we were tormented by it. We decided that we wanted to make something of our lives. AMIE (engineering) examinations could be taken as a private candidate.[1] We had picked up the forms. But I didn't have enough money to pay the fees and ended up not filling out the form. Vijay insisted: "Come on, fill it out, I will borrow money from my father." I refused. So once again my ambition for higher education came to naught.

Jabalpur changed me. My speech patterns changed. My manners also changed. I made many friends who were deeply interested in contemporary issues and constantly argued about them. I took part in seminars and cultural functions. I became involved in the literary life of Jabalpur. I also began to develop my own views about literature. I was more attracted to social realism than to aestheticist and formalist types of writings.

Pitaji's letters from the village persistently asked me to agree to get married. He felt that I was getting too old. By my age men became fathers. I kept refusing to get married. I wanted to stay away from the hassles of family life. My younger sister, Maya, who was two years younger than I, had been married off three years earlier.

I had been extremely busy for the last two years. My training was proceeding well. On the matter of caste, hostel life wasn't too bad. At times, however, the students from Delhi and Muradnagar made remarks. Other than those from Dehra Dun and Meerut, no one knew what my caste was, although I had adopted "Valmiki" as my last name.[2] Many people in the institute became my intimates. Shri Lalji always invited me to his home. And I learned a lot from Prakash Kamble.

---

1. Eligible candidates who need not be registered with an academc institution are considered by the board holding the examinations to be "private" candidates.

2. Castes are local and regional, so outsiders cannot tell exactly what one's caste is.

The Ordnance Factory Training Institute in Bombay called for applicants for draftsman training. Almost all the students at our institute applied. Candidates were to be chosen on the basis of an India-wide competition. On the basis of my written examination, I was asked to come to Bombay to appear for the oral. Once again financial problems reared their heads. Vijay gave me some money. Only then was I able to leave for Bombay to appear for the interview.

I received the call from Bombay just as I was finishing my training at Khamaria. Although I did feel happy, my family's dire economic straits dominated my thoughts. The chances of finding employment immediately after training were excellent. Finding employment meant an improvement of our economic situation. I needed the job to make a living. To go for two and a half years' further training seemed impossible. I talked about my circumstances to Mr. Thomas, a senior lecturer at the institute. He listened to me seriously and said, "If you have managed this long, try to manage for another two and a half years. After the Ambernath, Bombay, training, you will be in a better financial position." He also gave me a hundred rupees. I said repeatedly, "No, sir, I won't take these rupees," but he was insistent. "Keep them. Bombay is a big city. You will need them. Return them when you get a job."

Yashpal Kalia, a senior trainee, also gave me one hundred rupees. Only because of these two hundred rupees did I manage to reach Bombay.

I left Vijay Bahadur Soul in Jabalpur and went to Bombay. Leaving him behind was heartbreaking. We had been inseparable for the last three years. Vijay's eyes were also filled with tears. My relationship with Vijay was deep. I felt incomplete without him. For me Vijay Bahadur Soul was even more important than my own kith and kin.

I had collected a lot of books while staying in the hostel. I did not have the means to take them to Bombay with me. I had a friend named Karan Singh at the vehicle factory in Jabalpur. Vijay and I had stayed at his place for some time. I left my entire collection with him before leaving for Bombay. He promised to send the books to Bombay through somebody. But the way things turned out, I never managed to return to Jabalpur, nor did Karan Singh send those books to Bombay. We corresponded for some time. But after a while even the correspondence ceased. Karan Singh and Vijay Soul had no interest in these literary books of mine. For them, they carried no greater value than old junk. Among these books was that copy of Sara Aakash that a stranger had left for me in the desk drawer.

On the evening of July 8, 1970, I arrived at the hostel of the Ordnance Factory Training Institute with my meager belongings. The institute's van was standing outside Kalyan station. Many others had also come from Jabalpur. The hostel was at a scenic spot, at the foot of Ambernath Hill. Among the ordnance factories, this institute and its hostel hold a special place. The technicians trained here are counted among the best technicians and draftsmen. The evenings in the hostel were lively. Along with facilities for gymnastics and indoor games, the hostel had a swimming pool and a library. I was greatly excited when I saw the library. In that library I read Pasternak, Hemingway, Victor Hugo, Pierre Louis, Tolstoy, Pearl Buck, Turgenev, Dostoyevsky, Stevenson, Oscar Wilde, Romain Rolland, and Émile Zola. That was where I read the entire works of Rabindranath Tagore and Kalidasa.[3]

Ten students lived in each room in the hostel. With me were Sudama Patil (a Maharashtrian from Bhusaval), V. K. Upadhyay (from Kanpur), P. C. Mridha (a Bengali), K. C. Roy (a Bengali), Dilip Kumar Mitra (a Bengali), B. K. John (from Katni in Madhya Pradesh), Gaur Mohan Das (a Bengali from Calcutta), and Gulati

---

3. Kalidasa, who lived in about the fifth century A.D., was the greatest figure in classical Sanskrit literature. He wrote plays—Shakuntala, Vikramorvasi, and Malavikagnimitra survive—as well as fine epic and lyric poetry.

(a Sikh). Sudama Patil and I soon became fast friends. He was also a connoisseur of literature. He loved theater. Every Saturday and Sunday both of us went to Bombay to see plays. Once in a while, if there was a good show in the middle of the week, we would sneak out. The hostel was locked at ten every night. One could get caught while scaling down the wall. Many a time we got into the hostel through the path by the drain.

One day I happened across the gate key. I went to the factory and cut myself a spare. As soon as we had the spare key, our problem was solved.

But we were caught one day. The guard used to fall asleep by midnight on the veranda of the library. We would quietly unlock the gate and enter. Once inside, we would lock the gate again. That day the guard happened to be awake. He shouted when he saw us unlocking the gate. The lock was already open, and we were inside.

He threatened to complain to the warden. I asked him, "What will you complain about?"

"That you came in from outside after unlocking the gate," he said.

I scolded him. "We did not come from the outside. We were inside. You had forgotten to lock the gate. Now lock it."

We began to argue heatedly. The warden, Upadhyay, heard us, and he too came to the gate. When he saw me, he said "Maharshi, what are you doing here?"[4]

With great self-assurance I said, "Warden Sahib, this guard forgot to lock the gate. See, the lock is still open. I was trying to explain this to him but he doesn't agree."

That day we got away with it somehow. But the warden suspected both of us. We had to put a halt to our activities for the time being.

The famous actor Shriram Lagoo was appearing in a play staged at Ambernath's Gandhi School. We managed to get the

---

4. Maharshi means great sage, someone who impresses by his wisdom and ethical standards.

tickets for the play after much running around. Shriram Lagoo's role as *nat samrat* [best actor; literally, the emperor of the theater], was on everyone's lips. We left the hostel quietly after eating dinner in the mess. The play started at 9:30 P.M. and it was already 9:15 P.M. Patil and I were rushing along the road to the station. Suddenly, we saw Upadhyayji coming from the opposite direction. He saw us.

"Maharshi, where are you off to at this time?" he said reprovingly.

We looked at each other's face. Suddenly, Patil spoke up. "Sir, I have a headache. We are going to the station to have some tea or coffee. We will be back right after drinking a cup."

"Why? Don't you get tea and coffee in the mess?"

"We do, sir. But today there wasn't any milk in the mess. That's why we are going to the station," Patil improvised.

Upadhyayji said, "Come with me, I'll get you some coffee." He brought us to his home. The tickets for the play were squirming in our pockets. We couldn't figure out how to get him off our backs.

After seating us in the drawing room, he asked his wife to make the coffee and sat on the sofa across from us. I looked at Patil from the corner of my eye. He was smiling.

As soon as Mrs. Upadhyay entered the kitchen, I got up and said, "Ammaji [Mother], Warden Sahib is bothering you unnecessarily. I will make the coffee."

She was pleased to see me. "Maharshi, you go sit—I will make it."

I went up to her and whispered. "Ammaji, both of us were going to the Gandhi School to see a play. Warden Sahib waylaid us and brought us here. See, here are the tickets, but he doesn't know anything."

Ammaji examined me from head to toe. "I see. Is it a good play?"

I said, "Ammaji, it is very good."

"Then why don't you go?" she said with a laugh.

"How can we go? Warden Sahib won't give us permission," I whispered.

She came into the drawing room. "Listen, what kind of a war-

den are you? Why don't you let the young people go and have some
fun? Go, Maharshi, but don't be too late."

Upadhyayji had not been allowed to put his foot down. We
both ran out and didn't stop until we got to the Gandhi School.
The play had already started. It ended at 1 A.M. The guard had
gone to sleep, leaving the gate unlocked. Sudama locked the gate,
proclaiming, "Jai Ammaji!"[5]

During those days we saw Vijay Tendulkar's Marathi plays,
Sakharam Binder, Gidhare, and *Khamosh Adalat Jari Hai.* The
Theatre Unit's *Haivadan* and *Asharh ka Ek Din* were enlivened by
the acting of Amrish Puri, Amol Palekar, Sunila Pradhan, and
Sulabha Desphande.[6] We also organized a drama group in the
hostel. We started rehearsals. We staged our plays in many venues
in Ambernath.

At about that time the terrible incident involving the blinding
of two brothers occurred in Poona. In a village near Poona some
upper-caste people blinded the Ganwai brothers, and tension in
the Bombay-Poona area was great. The Dalit Panthers had started their activities. Making the Ganwai brothers my starting point,
I sent an essay on the problems of Dalits to the *Navbharat Times* in
Bombay, and the editors published it. This essay aroused a lot of
controversy. The government employees who were Shiv Sena supporters complained about my article to the principal of the institute, Shri Desai.[7]

The principal called me to his office and put a copy of the
newspaper in front of me. "You have written this?" he asked.

"Ji."

He asked a second time, "Look carefully. This article is by you?"

"Ji, it is mine," I owned up.

---

5. Long live Ammaji!

6. All are among the most famous actors and actresses in India.

7. The Shiv Sena is a right-wing political party of upper-caste Maharashtrians. The
Shiv Sena opposes the migration of people from other states to Bombay and sup-
ports upper-caste dominance. It is also anti-Muslim.

"You are in a government institution. There could be disciplinary action against you on the basis of this article."

I kept quiet. After a while he spoke again. "Don't do all this during training—you will be thrown out. Go now. Be careful in the future." He let me go after giving this oral warning. But the behavior of some students changed toward me after the publication of the article. Because I had shown empathy toward the Dalits, they began to research my caste. To show sympathy to Dalits was a crime in their eyes.

Sudama Patil translated Acharya Atre's Marathi play, *Maruchi Mavshi*. I was given the lead role in it. After the first performance the people of Ambernath began to recognize me as an actor. Instead of calling me Omprakash Valmiki, they would call me by the character's name. I was beginning to feel a stirring inside me. While working on Atre's play, I became acquainted with Kulkarni, the distinguished actor-director of Ambernath's Marathi theater. We soon became close friends. I got the opportunity to work with several well-known directors.

While I was groping to work out a path for myself, Pitaji's letters repeated the same message: I want to see you married. I used to send a fixed sum to Pitaji every month out of my stipend. After paying my mess dues, I had little left for out-of-pocket expenses. We got theater tickets at student rates, and we learned ways to travel ticketless on trains. We devised many formulas to trick the ticket checkers of Dadar, V.T., and Churchgate. We toured around Bombay without spending much money.

During that period I was introduced to Marathi Dalit literature. Dalit writings were changing the face of Marathi literature. The words of Daya Pawar, Namdev Dhasal, Raja Dhale, Gangadhar Pantavane, Baburao Bagul, Keshav Meshram, Narayan Surve, Vaman Nimbalkar, and Yashwant Manohar were igniting sparks in my veins. Their voices exhilarated me, filled me with new energy. My reading of Dalit literature was beginning to change my notions about what is literature. Sudama Patil was my helper and guide in this quest. My knowledge of Marathi was gradually increasing.

Govind Maurya arrived from Jabalpur in the next batch of students who were accepted at the institute. Now we were a three-some. The three of us together combed through all the bookstores in Bombay that carried Hindi books. I had become friends with the owner of Hindi Granth Ratnakar. We went to Hindi Granth Ratnakar at least once a month.

Vijay Shankar, Narendra Gogia, Amit Aggarwal, and Rajesh Vajpai also joined our group. Along with the technical education of our training, this new world of literature was filling us with a new consciousness. We experienced the bitter and insurmountable realities of life even during the fun-filled days of hostel life. Our classmates ran off to the cinema and picnics as soon as classes were over. We spent long hours debating life's serious problems. We joined all those activities that accelerated social transformation. Often Vijay Shankar would say, "Hey, fellows, you don't seem to have ever been young."

Youth had a different mind-set in the hostel, and we did not fit into it because useless things like literature had deranged our brains.

Patil had a friend named Ramesh who was also from Bhusaval. He had introduced us to Kulkarni. Vinayak Sadashiv Kulkarni lived in a flat in the colony [neighborhood]. He was at the center of all cultural activities that took place in and around Ambernath. We became close after only a couple of meetings. Often we would go to his flat in the evening. Kulkarni was fond of eating meat and fish. It was impossible for him to cook it in his own kitchen, which was a vegetarian one as befitted his status as a Maharashtrian Brahmin, and he would therefore often come to the mess to eat the meat cooked for Sunday lunch. He was con-siderably older than we were. His younger daughter, Savita, who was a college student, was the same age as I.

Because Kulkarni ate at our mess every Sunday, Patil's and my mess bills went up. I had to send money to Pitaji out of my stipend. Patil's financial situation was quite similar to mine. Although he was slightly better off than I, he had two younger brothers studying in college and he needed to support them. Both of us lived quite frugally, yet we were always scrounging. I was also short of clothes. Kulkarni's meals in our mess every Sunday were a drastic blow to our finances. Sudama Patil moaned one day: "This Brahmin invites himself every Sunday!"

We spent our evenings at Kulkarni's house, but we always ate dinner at the mess.

Sudama Patil believed in prayer and fasting. He went regularly to the temple. Ambernath has a beautiful ancient temple of the god Shiva. Patil would go to this temple twice a week. I had no interest in religion. Ambedkar and Marxist literature had changed my consciousness. I would go with Patil up to the temple and sit on the culvert's ledge. The temple complex and its quiet surroundings were pleasant.

Often Mrs. Kulkarni came to the temple with Savita. Many a time we came upon them in the temple complex. One day Savita came and sat beside me on the ledge. Mrs. Kulkarni had gone inside the temple. "Why don't you go inside the temple?" Savita asked in a light tone.

"I have no faith in these stone idols," I replied frankly.

She was sitting very close to me, and I felt a strange sensation. She insisted, "Come on, let us go in the temple. Sudama Dada is in there too."

"Yes, Patil is inside. You go in as well. I am fine here," I tried to stall her. She became very quiet. After some time she asked, "Why are you so quiet all the time?"

"I like listening," I replied jovially. She burst out laughing. Her laugh was like the tinkle of temple bells. All of a sudden, she asked, "Do you see films?"

"Yes . . . sometimes."

"Will you come with me to a film?" she asked, wrapping her arm around mine. I replied in a noncommittal way that I would let her know after asking Sudama Patil.

Savita became upset. "Why? Can't we go by ourselves?" That day I had heard a waterfall gurgling somewhere in my heart. I was a reserved person and my family's conservative values ruled me. I had not even dreamed of a romantic relationship with a girl like her because the many barriers between us held me back. But many such small incidents had signaled to me that she was attracted to me. She had started to visit us in the hostel as well. Sudama forbade her from coming to the hostel. Sometimes he even scolded her. But Sudama's prohibitions made no difference to her. She would go around looking into my books when she came to our room. Sometimes she would pick up the books scattered around the room and arrange them neatly. As a vegetarian, she did not care for the mess food.

A day before the Diwali festival, on *chaturdashi*, the fourth day of worship, Mrs. Kulkarni invited me to their home. And I was to be there at four in the morning. When I asked Patil about it, he burst out laughing. I did not understand the reason for his laughter and when I demanded an explanation, he said, "Enjoy yourself. Mrs. Kulkarni is going to bathe and massage you with fragrant oils."

"What?" I asked, utterly surprised.

Patil told me about the traditions of Maharashtrian Brahmins. The women of the family massage and bathe the male family members in the sacred morning hour on *chaturdashi*. I asked him if he was also going. He said that they hadn't invited him.

I slept fitfully that night. On the one hand, I had to get there by 4 A.M., on the other I had an argument raging inside me. The Kulkarnis' overtures were attractive to me, yet I was hesitant because of my family circumstances.

Three low stools had been placed on their veranda. Kulkarni, Ajay [Kulkarni's son], and I sat down on them. My mind kept remembering the stifling atmosphere of my village. Mrs. Kulkarni massaged the three of us with a fragrant herbal paste and oil. The oil had a wonderful smell. I had wrapped a towel on top of my underwear. Mrs. Kulkarni told me to put away the towel. I said I felt awkward. Mrs. Kulkarni snatched the towel away from me. She said, "You are like my son, Ajay. Why should you feel awkward?" At that moment my heart filled with emotion. I thought of Ma, who had been ill for some time.

The soft maternal touch of Mrs. Kulkarni's hand reminded me of the touch of Ma's calloused hands. Sitting by my pillow, when Ma ran her fingers through my hair, I would drop off to sleep peacefully.

Mrs. Kulkarni bathed me in hot water in the bathroom. I was besieged by a fear: What would happen if these people found out that I was born in the untouchable Chuhra caste?

The blinding of the Ganwai brothers near Poona was in the news. The Dalits of Bombay-Poona area had risen up in a powerful protest.

The Kulkarni family had given me unstinting affection. They never made me feel like an outsider. But Savita's attraction toward me was making me fearful. I felt unsettled whenever I met her. The closer Savita tried to come, the faster I ran.

One day I met Professor Kamble at the Kulkarnis' place. Kulkarni and Kamble were deep in conversation about Marathi plays. Patil and I were listening to them quietly. Mrs. Kulkarni came in with the tea. While drinking my tea, I noticed Kamble's cup. It was different from the cups offered to the rest of us. I asked Sudama Patil, who nudged me to be quiet. On our way back I asked him again. At first he tried to be evasive but finally he said, "Maharashtrian Brahmins, especially those from Poona, don't allow Mahars to touch their dishes.[8] That's why their dishes are kept separate. Mrs. Kulkarni had come to take the used cups of everybody else, but Kulkarni had taken Kamble's cup inside."

As I listened to him, my ears started to boil as though someone had poured mercury into them. "Do they treat all Dalits like that?" I wanted to know.

My village was divided along lines of touchability and untouchability. The situation was bad in Dehra Dun and in Uttar

---

8. Mahar is an untouchable caste in Maharashtra to which Ambedkar also belonged.

Pradesh in general at this time. When I saw well-educated people
in a metropolitan city like Bombay indulging in such behavior, I
felt a fountain of hot lava erupting within me. "Yes, that is how
they behave with all Dalits," Patil replied frankly. He respected
Babasaheb Ambedkar and supported Dalit protest movements.
Although he was an upper-caste person, he was not narrow-mind-
ed. A storm was rising inside me. The incident had unsettled me
deeply. I asked Patil, "Do they know about me?"

"Perhaps not . . . perhaps they think Valmiki is a Brahmin surname.[9] Maybe that's why they invited you for the Diwali bath."
Patil was becoming somewhat serious.

"You never told them?" I asked heatedly.

"Why should I have? Is it a crime to be a Dalit?" Patil retort-
ed angrily.

"What if they find out tomorrow?" I objected.

"So? How are you to blame? If they didn't ask you, why should
you get a drummer to announce your caste? Yes, if they had
inquired and you had lied in order to be admitted to their circle,
then you would be worthy of blame," Patil replied firmly.

I couldn't get back to normal after this incident. My restlessness tormented me. I find it difficult to survive in such stifling
environments, where everything seems false. I did not hide my
inner torment from Patil, who tried to talk me out of it. "The
entire value system of the Brahmins is based on lies and deception.
Forget about it and have fun," he would say.

I did not crave for love and respect gained on the basis of a lie.
I remained mired in turmoil. Lost in my inner battle, I did not visit
the Kulkarnis for several days. Savita came to the hostel after waiting in vain for my visit. I wanted to talk to Savita frankly. But it
wasn't possible within the four walls of the hostel. I said to Savita,
"I need to talk to you—alone."

---

9. This is a reference to the poet Valmiki of the third century B.C.. Although Valmiki
was lower caste, some Brahmins use that name because of the sacred nature of the
epic.

"Alone? . . . Why?" she had replied mischievously, her eyes dancing.

"Hmm."

"Let us go to the temple tomorrow."

"But won't your mother be there with you?" I objected.

"No, I will come alone," she assured me.

After Savita left, I told Patil that I was going to tell Savita everything. Patil tried to stop me; he said, "No, don't do that. It will cause a storm."

But I had come to a decision. Things should be cleared up. I would face whatever happened.

Savita met me near the Upkar restaurant at the Ambernath train station. She wore a white skirt-and-blouse outfit that greatly suited her milky-fair complexion. Her eyes were sparkling and her walk had a spring in it. She talked nonstop as usual. I was replying briefly with ohs and yeses. I did not know how to tell her, where to begin.

Suddenly, Savita reacted as though she had remembered something. "Oh, I had almost forgotten, weren't you going to tell me something?" Her eyes grew large as she gazed at me steadily. For a moment I felt I wouldn't be able to do it.

Gathering my courage, I said, "That day when Professor Kamble came to your place . . ."

Before I could finish Savita interrupted with, "That Mahar . . . SC?"[10]

The way she said it made me flush with anger, "Yes, the same," I replied bitterly.

Surprised, Savita asked, "Why are you thinking of this today?"

My voice hardened, "You had served him tea in a different cup?"

"Yes, the SCs and the Muslims who come to our house, we keep their dishes separate," Savita replied evenly.

---

10. SC is the abbreviation for Scheduled Caste, and the acronym is often used in private upper-caste speech.

"Do you think this discrimination is right?" I asked. She felt the sharp edge in my voice now.

"Oh . . . why, are you mad? How can we feed them in the same dishes?"

"Why not? In the hotel . . . in the mess, everyone eats together. Then what is wrong in eating together in your home as well?" I tried to reason with her.

Savita defended the discrimination as right and justified by tradition. Her arguments were infuriating me. However, I remained calm. According to her, SCs were uncultured. Dirty.

I asked her, "How many SCs do you know? What is your personal experience in this regard?"

She fell silent. Her effervescence subsided. We sat on the ledge for a while. Then I asked her, "What do you think of me?"

"Aai and Baba praise you. They say you are very different from their preconceptions about Uttar Pradesh people," Savita cooed.[11]

"I asked for your opinion."

"I like you." She leaned on my arm.

I pushed her away and asked, "OK—would you like me even if I were an SC?"

"How can you be an SC?" she laughed.

"Why not? What if I am?" I had insisted.

"You are a Brahmin," she said with conviction.

"Who told you that?"

"My father."

"He is wrong. I am an SC." I put all my energy into those words. I felt that a fire had started inside me.

"Why do you say such things?" she said angrily.

"I am telling you the truth. I won't lie to you. I never claimed that I am a Brahmin."

She stared at me, totally shocked. She still thought that I was joking with her.

---

11. Northern Indians, including the people of Uttar Pradesh (the Northern State), where the author comes from, are generally considered by other Indians to be overly rough, macho, and aggressive.

I said as plainly as I could that I was born in a Chuhra family in Uttar Pradesh.

Savita appeared grave. Her eyes were filled with tears and she said tearfully, "You are lying, right?"

"No, Savi. It is the truth. You ought to know this." I had managed to convince her.

She started to cry, as though my being an SC was a crime. She sobbed for a long time. Suddenly, the distance between us had increased. The hatred of thousands of years had entered our hearts. What a lie culture and civilization are.

On the way back we were both quiet. Immersed in the uproar that was going on inside me, I could feel that the tension inside me was dissipating. It was as though a great burden had lifted off my chest. Crossing the railway line near the station, I said to Savita, "This is our last meeting."

"Why? Won't you come home?" She sounded surprised.

"No, I won't be able to come anymore."

She came to a standstill. She said, "Whether you visit our home or not, don't tell my father if what you told me is true." She looked as if she were going to cry. Her voice broke.

"But why not?" I wanted to know.

"Promise me you won't tell him," Savita's eyes entreated me.

We never met again. After some days I was transferred to Chandrapur, Maharashtra. I left without visiting them. Suddenly, all links had snapped. After the training I was appointed to the ordnance factory in Chanda (Chandrapur).

NOW I WAS WORKING at the ordnance factory in Chandrapur. During the first few days after my arrival, I stayed with Dinesh Vajpayi and Anand Sharma. Afterward, I was allotted a room in the hostel, which I had to share with Jaikishan Jaiswal. Jaiswal showed some hesitancy in the beginning, but it gradually disappeared. We lived together in that room for quite some time.

It took me awhile to understand factory life and adjust to it. I studied in my spare time after work. The theater and the literary scene were vibrant there. Nonetheless, most inhabitants were quite traditional in their thinking. Many Hindi writers lived in Chandrapur, and I was beginning to come in contact with them.

In 1974, with the help of a few friends, I started a theater group called Meghdoot Natya Sanstha. Soon this group became well known around Nagpur for its engaged perspective. A campaign had begun with regular shows and street plays to acquaint the wider public about contemporary issues. A team of brave young men was devoting itself fully to this task.

The country was resounding with J.P.'s movement.[1] I had written some good poems at last, poems that weren't just rhymes, and people were beginning to recognize me as a poet through my

---

1. Jaya Prakash Narayan (1902–79) was a Gandhian, socialist, and peasant leader who spent many years in jail under the British. He formed a protest movement that won widespread support against corruption in politics, coming into direct conflict with the then prime minister, Indira Gandhi, whose resignation he called for. In retaliation she had many of her opponents arrested, and she declared a state of emergency, which meant abrogating the Constitution. He led the political coalition that defeated her yet refused the post of prime minister for himself.

poems in *Navbharat, Yugharm,* and *Nai Dunia.* I had also begun to write a column in a Chandrapur weekly called *Janapratinidhi.*

During my Chandrapur days I absorbed the strongest currents of the Dalit movement. In this part of the country I came across the marvelous glow of Dalit consciousness. The self-fulfillment that I experienced in connecting with the Dalit movement was a truly unique experience for me. The deeper my involvement became with the movement, the further many of my friends moved away from me. In their eyes I had wandered away from the right path and was bent on destroying my talent and creativity.

Buddha's philosophy on human freedom attracted me. He says that there is no such thing as the unchangeable in a constantly changing universe. The human being alone matters. Compassion and wisdom are what take a person toward transcendence. Nagpur's Dikshabhumi is a place of pilgrimage for Dalits. Here I met Bhadant Anand Kaushalyayan. Kaushalyayanji removed my doubts about Buddhism through sustained argument. I also met Bhau Samarth at his home in Nagpur. He was a simple and unassuming person, a poet, a painter, and a true human being. Whenever we met, we met with great openness. We met only a few times but all our meetings are forever cherished in my heart.

Pitaji's latest letter said that he wanted to marry me off as soon as possible. Jasbir had found a match for me. But I was adamant—I hadn't yet settled down properly. Pitaji's harping about my marriage was making me feel as though I was entangled in thorny bushes. Tired of their pestering, in the end I was able to do what I wanted. I was able to refuse to marry the girl Jasbir had selected for me, and I married Swarnlata Bhabhi's younger sister Chanda, on December 27, 1973. That I was able to do so was the result of a struggle with my family.

One day a letter came from Pitaji. "Ma is ill. Come home soon." I left for home immediately. All the way I thought of Ma, worrying about how ill she was. As soon as I got off the bus at the bus terminal, I made a dash for home. I breathed a sigh of relief when I saw that she was all right. I asked her, "You were ill?"

Ma put her hand on my head and said, "The news of my illness has brought you home at last."

"What was so urgent that you called me in this way?" I asked, trying to control my anger.

"Your brother has settled a match for you. Now you get married. Who knows when my eyes will close," she said, trying to reason with me.

I listened to her silently but I was in turmoil. Jasbir had fixed a match for me without bothering to ask whether I was willing. Pitaji agreed with Jasbir. He had me cornered. They didn't want to hear any of my arguments. I found out after coming home that my mother's brother was behind this match. He wanted to tie this noose around me so that I would never be able to get out of his clutches.

I left Jasbir in the village and suddenly took off for Dehra Dun. I asked my cousin Surjan, "Have you seen the girl?" He refused to get dragged into the matter, and his wife, Swarnlata Bhabhi, was also evasive. Their attitude made me very upset. Hemlal was still a regular visitor at Surjan's place. In fact, he had become even closer to Surjan after I had left Dehra Dun for further training. It was Hemlal who made me suspicious of the match that my family had arranged for me. He was aware of the conspiracy that they had hatched. At first he said nothing, but after much prodding from me he told me about Uncle's role in the conspiracy.

I felt hopeless in my agony. After returning to the village, all I said to Jasbir was, "I want to see the girl." At that time our community didn't have the custom of showing the prospective bride. The elders decided it all. And the boy and the girl would go along with their decision. No one in the boy's family would go to see the girl. It was considered impolite. The mediator was trusted. Many a time this trust had led to horrible tragedies.

My demand was like a bombshell. Everyone was staring at me,

their eyes popping with astonishment. Jasbir agreed to my demand after a prolonged, heated argument. He and I left for Dehra Dun together. The girl was staying with her maternal uncle at the time. As soon as we got to Dehra Dun, we were informed that the girl had gone to her mother's place in Muzaffarnagar. Jasbir and I then went to Muzaffarnagar, but when we got there we were told that she was back in Dehra Dun. This was just a ploy not to show the girl to us. I felt ensnared in a bizarre situation. Very alone. I had no one, either in my family or in the outside world, with whom I could unravel the knots inside my heart. Even my sister-in-law, Swarnlata, Surjan's wife, had abandoned me to my own devices.

I returned to Chandrapur, depressed and lonely. I felt low for a long time after this visit home. Jasbir's letters kept coming with great frequency. He told me repeatedly that I was playing with his honor. How dare I flout the rules of our caste, our community? Education did not mean that one should stop obeying the hallowed customs of our people. Every letter of Jasbir's left a deep wound. I wanted to become something before getting married. And these people were coming after me with no holds barred.

I decided to bring things to an end. I went straight to Dehra Dun, taking Jasbir by surprise. He introduced me to the mother of the girl; she was visiting Dehra Dun at the time. She seemed like a nice, simple woman to me. She was happy to meet me. After meeting her, I felt even more confused. I again asked Jasbir to let me see the girl. But he said, "Don't you trust me? You have met the mother, what else do you want?"

"It's not the mother but the daughter that I am marrying," I said, boiling over. Jasbir and I did not speak to each other for three days. On the fourth day I met Swarnlata Bhabhi's sister, Chandrakala, also called Chanda. Telling her about everything in detail, I also told her what was in my heart, "Will you marry me?" Chanda was studying for her intermediate then. Surprise was written all over her face, and she asked, "What are you saying?"

"Think about it and let me know," I said confidently and left. The next day Chanda went to her older sister's home. The children [the sister's children], Seema, Rajiv, and Vinita, were very small then; Vinita was still a baby.

Chanda asked me in a whisper, "You're not joking, are you?"

"Absolutely not," I said.

"Will your brothers and father agree?" she asked doubtfully.

"Leave it to me," I replied calmly.

The next day I left for the village and talked to Pitaji. He came around after protesting a little. He had one condition. He said, "You must worship the pig before the marriage."

I refused point-blank. I don't believe in worshipping any deities. Pitaji was angry. My disbelief was an attack on his faith, and he wasn't willing to forgive me for that. Up until now he had not pressured me to participate in the ceremonies of worship, perhaps thinking that my resistance was caused by my youthful immaturity. But now he became enraged when he saw that I was protesting even at an important occasion like my marriage. He remained angry until the very end. I was absolutely determined not to give in.

I got married to Chanda, and despite his protestations Pitaji accepted her as my wife.[2] Uncle was angry, and Jasbir was on his side. Surjan was angry because I was marrying his sister-in-law. Uncle tried to prevent my marriage to Chanda, using Hemlal as a pawn. But Hemlal failed. The ties of our friendship were broken and scattered. I was sorry that I had lost a close friend.

After we were married, I took Chanda to Chandrapur. Our biggest problem was finding a house; I hadn't yet been allotted one in the government colony. I lived in the hostel and Jaikishan Jaiswal was my roommate. I wrote to my friend Ajay Sinha, who had been a roommate for a long time many years earlier [and who lived in Chandrapur]. He wrote back, "Bring your wife. We will arrange something."

---

2. Valmiki's father was angry because the author was breaking custom and had foiled the family's efforts to arrange an advantageous match on its own terms. Chanda would be of the same caste, because her sister's marriage, to Surjan, who is Valmiki's cousin, had been traditional.

Sukkhan Singh was in Delhi. He lived in R. K. Puram [a neighborhood]. We had studied together up to the intermediate level at Tyagi Inter College. After several years of searching for a job, he had found one at the Survey of India. He booked berths for us on the Dakshin Express.

I sent telegrams to Ajay Sinha and Suraj Khartar, informing them about the date and time of our arrival. But when the train arrived at Chandrapur at ten at night, no one was at the station to receive us. I had hoped that they would come with the factory van. At that time of night we had no chance of getting a bus to the ordnance factory. Anyway, we had a lot of luggage with us to set up our household, and it would have been difficult to load it onto the last bus, which was always crowded.

We spent the night in the waiting room of Chandrapur railway station. The stationmaster himself unlocked the room for us, advising us to rest. The station was pretty empty by that time. Few passengers had disembarked there. We caught the first bus in the morning and arrived at the ordnance factory estate. Leaving our luggage in the hostel, Chanda and I went to Suraj Khartar's quarters. He had already left for work. Chanda stayed there with his wife, Sushila, and I too went to the office. My leave had come to an end.

When Suraj found that I had left Chanda at his house, he was very happy. Khartar and I were quite close. He was from Ballarshah, near Chandrapur. He was a wonderful human being. He had an openness about him that attracted me tremendously. We spent one night with Suraj and Sushila Bhabhi. The next day we were going to shift to Ajay Sinha's quarters. He came to meet Chanda that evening.

Suraj and Sushila Bhabhi welcomed Chanda with great warmth. Before we left for Ajay's place, Chanda took a new sari out of her box and presented it to Sushila Bhabhi. But she refused to accept it. I respected Sushila Bhabhi greatly, and Chanda wanted to show her respect by giving the sari as a present. Her refusal spoiled everything in a second. Chanda looked at me in surprise. I said humbly, "Bhabhiji, if you don't like this sari, select another one." But she went and sat in the next room. She wasn't saying anything, either.

When I asked Suraj about it, all he said was, "Just ignore her. Don't feel upset by her behavior. Begin your married life on a positive note." My eyes filled up with tears. We left for Ajay's flat. Suraj came with us to drop us off. Sushila Bhabhi's behavior had upset us all.

I tried to maintain normal relations with Sushila Bhabhi. To this day we have no idea what Chanda did or said that upset her so much. Suraj would often come to meet Chanda and would bring his son, Apratim, but our visits to their place became fewer and fewer.

Ajay Sinha gave his flat to us and went to live with Anand Sharma, whose wife had gone to her parents' place to await the birth of her child. Then Ajay's marriage was arranged and he went to Benares. While the news of his marriage made me happy, I was also a bit worried that we would now have to vacate his flat. Ajay reassured me before he left for Benares, saying, "Valmiki, don't worry at all. If you don't find a place before I return, then we will all live together. You two can take one room and we will take the other. We will do the cooking together." His words had lightened my anxiety.

I found a place after much running around. A two-room flat was allotted to me, a 31-C, type 2, in sector 5, quite close to Ajay's flat. We moved in a week before their return. Ajay and his wife came directly to us after their marriage, and they lived with us for several days. Those were simply wonderful days! The relationship that developed between Ajay and me then, its sweetness, still lingers in my memories. Mrs. Sinha was also very courteous and affectionate, an unassuming, easy-going person. My life has gone through many ups and downs, but my high regard for them has never been clouded.

I had always dreamed of doing social work among the Dalits, and during my time in Chandrapur I was able to put my plans into practice. In Maharashtra the groundwork done by Ambedkar and Jotirao Phooley inspired thousands upon thousands to join the struggle. This intellectual revolution provided a new dimension to my writing.

A magazine called *Him Jharna* [Frozen Waterfall] had been started in Chandrapur. Its editor was Jagdish Rahi. He had published many issues when the magazine suddenly folded. Rahi was a close friend of mine. He was also a good singer. Something had happened and he lost his job at the coal mine. When his job went, so did the magazine, and one day Jagdish Rahi packed up and left Chandrapur. All that was left was the memory of those moments when we had listened to his songs and made plans to bring out a great Hindi magazine in Chandrapur. We had worked together. We had stayed up nights to correct the proofs. In that city of blistering heat only a dynamic person like Rahi, bursting with the sap of life, could imagine a magazine like *Him Jharna*.

A Marathi poet, Loknath Yashwant, also came back to live in Chandrapur. He often came to visit us at the Ordnance Factory Colony. We attended several functions in the city together. He was a rather shy person, very ideologically committed. Friends like him made me feel at home in Chandrapur. Amarnath Verma created a bond that went deeper than friendship. He became like a member of the family, declaring himself to be Chanda's elder brother, and would often address me as "Jijaji." All these friends were precious to me. The affection that Padma Bhabhi gave Chanda and me is a treasure that will last a whole lifetime. Chandrapur has given me many friends who are closer to me than my own kith and kin, and I am incomplete without my friends. Their affection and faith have given me the strength and the inspiration to go forward.

In 1978 the Dalit Panthers organized a huge rally in Bombay, demanding that Marathwada University's name be changed to Dr. Ambedkar University. Dalit Panther activists from all over Maharashtra gathered in front of Bombay's legislative assembly.

The state assembly passed the bill for the name change. *Savarnas,*
or upper-caste people, had opposed the bill on a large scale, and
rioting and destruction of public property occurred in several
towns and cities. Ahmadnagar, Aurangabad. Nagpur, Sholapur,
Bombay, Nasik, and Amravati were tense. Marathwada felt the
effects of the rioting the most. Dalit neighborhoods were
torched. Hundreds of people died. The news in the papers broke
one's heart.

The name change had become a selfhood issue for Dalits.
Nagpur saw incidents of violence. Protesters had also marched in
Chandrapur.

The Maharashtra government withdrew the name-change
bill. The Dalits were disappointed. They did not lose heart, however, and were working relentlessly to keep the issue in the public
eye. They channeled all their energy into the movement. The
inspiring leadership and impassioned speeches of Bapu Rav Jagtap
and Jogendra Kavare kept Dalits fired up.

The hatred of thousands of years was once again visible in its
original form. I saw this movement of Dalit assertion from close
up. Each follicle of my body felt the heat of the movement. The
cruel social arbiters of Indian society were denying individual
merit. In their eyes Ambedkar was simply a Mahar, and they could
not care less if his scholarship was as vast as the sky.

The battle for Dalit selfhood that Ambedkar had fought in
his life had unleashed the flow of self-confidence among the
Dalits. He had created the Republican Party to participate in the
political process, but the party had splintered into several groups
after his death. Every leader, declaring himself to be Babasaheb's
[Ambedkar's] heir, had joined the race to become the party's pres-
ident. As a result, each created his own party. In Maharashtra,
Dalit Panthers had given a new direction to the Dalit movement.
The leaders and activists of the Dalit Panthers were trying out a
new experiment by combining Marxism and Ambedkarism. The
whole of Maharashtra felt the glow of this new burst of Dalit
power. This experiment, however, was to fizzle out badly.

The writers who came out of the Dalit Panthers brought a new mood to Marathi Dalit literature. This literature was more vital, more progressive, than canonical Marathi literature. It was modern in the true sense of the word.

———

Protests against the reservation of quotas became grim in Gujarat, where the antireservationists had committed horrendous violence in the rural areas. The *tandav* dance of violence carried on in all directions.[3] The antireservationists stood under Gandhi's statues in places like Baroda and Gandhinagar and vented their hatred for Dalits. Their poison began to make inroads in Maharashtra as well. The harassment of Dalits in government and government-funded workplaces increased. *Savarnas* had hastily created straw organizations like the Shoshit Workers Union that were conspiring against Dalits in a concerted manner.

All this created an atmosphere of overwhelming fear and terror, and not only Dalit workers but Dalit managers were living in fear. They did not have an organization. Because of the lack of communication among them, they faced their problems as isolated individuals. The lack of unity fractured their self-confidence. The Shoshit Workers Union, through its brochures and posters, was giving rise to an inferiority complex among Dalits. One brochure was also distributed at the ordnance factory in Chandrapur. It caused tremendous unease. All seemed quiet on the surface, but things were simmering underneath.

To remain quiet at such times means to erase oneself. Dalits organized a huge rally near the factory gate; the principal of the Central School, Shri Gondane; P. C. Kamble, a civil servant; and thousands of activists from various organizations participated. The protesters unanimously endorsed a motion to counteract the conspiracy of upper castes. Brochures that were distributed the

———

3. *Tandav* refers to an allusion to Lord Shiva's dance of destruction.

next day created an instant reaction. The managers of the factory took no action against the stuff that the Shoshit Workers distributed. But the moment Dalit brochures came out, the administration sprang to action. Officials called Dalit representatives in for questioning. After much arguing and protesting, the administration promised to take action against the propaganda that the antireservationists were circulating.

Sumthana village was the center of our activities. We held all our meetings there. That was where we formulated the strategy to neutralize the Shoshit Workers' plot in order to bolster the weakened morale of Dalit employees. The mutual goodwill among Dalits and other people had almost died. The communal and casteist forces had won the day.[4] They had sown the seeds of hatred among the employees, and even the organizations that shouted slogans like "Long Live Workers' Unity" were not been able to stop the hatred from sprouting.

The well of hatred between Dalits and non-Dalits has grown unabated, and no one seems to be trying to bridge it. When Dalits stand up to protect their selfhood, they are declared casteists. The dyed-in-the-wool casteists are actually the ones who make these declarations against Dalits. This is a move by the traditionalists and status-quoists, who are always suspicious of Dalits.

———

Looking at Maharashtra's Dalit *bastis*—both rural and urban— fills one's heart with sadness. Thanks to Ambedkar's consciousness raising among the Mahar *bastis*, Mahars had turned to education en masse. But Mangs and Mehtars and others were still illiterate. Dalit activists had plenty of pluck. Their resolve and activism filled one with hope. Even the activists, however, har-

———

4. By *communal* the author means community focused, which is a reference to ethnic or religious groups and their politics of antagonism; a casteist is someone who upholds the caste system.

bored feelings of caste differences. Although they talked outwardly of forgetting the differences between Mahars, Mangs, Chamars, and Mehtars, all untouchable castes, internally they were caught in the clutches of these beliefs. Whenever it became apparent that activists were reacting to such feelings, my heart would break. The hesitation of the activists when they entered the Mehtar *bastis* was apparent to anyone watching. It was also mostly the Mahars who attended Ambedkar's birth anniversary celebrations.

Babasaheb had converted to Buddhism. Mahars had converted along with him. But lots of families were still tied to the Hindu gods and goddesses. Babasaheb's message had not reached the Mehtar *bastis* at all. Whatever little had trickled in had come packed in a casteist mold. Whenever I talked about it with a Mehtar, he looked at me in surprise. Mehtars had respect for Babasaheb, but his followers had not been able to win their minds and hearts. They were Mehtars, placed at the very bottom of the social ladder. This feeling prevented them from joining the movement. They were suspicious of the Dalit leadership.

The internal contradictions of the Dalit movement have weakened it, and the consequences have been felt at the political level too.

There is no real difference between Maharashtra's Mehtars and Uttar Pradesh's Chuhra Valmikis; except for the language, everything else is similar. The Mehtars also breed pigs. They too make an offering of pig and liquor in the worship of their gods and goddesses. Their customs and traditions are pretty similar as well.

The centuries-old inferiority complex affected a segment of the Dalits, and this compelled them to hide their identity as Dalits. They kept their distance from other Dalits in order to win favor from the *savarnas*, and they worked against Dalits, reporting on their activities to the *savarnas*.

Residents of the Ordnance Factory Colony in Chandrapur celebrated Ambedkar's birth anniversary with great fanfare. I participated in it with great enthusiasm. We organized poetry readings, panel discussions, and art exhibitions and staged plays

and street theater. The *savarna* caste members of our organization, which was called Meghdoot Natya Sanstha, would
inevitably be very busy with some important matters at such
times. They disappeared from the scene during the Ambedkar
birth anniversary celebrations. Only during Ganesh Chaturthi,
Shivaji Jayanti, Janmashtami, and Ramnavami, all important fes-
tivals of the gods worshipped by the *savarnas,* did they work on
behalf of Meghdoot Natya Sanstha's endeavors. This behavior
exposed the internecine divisions among us. I wanted to discuss
these problems and contradictions, but they would avoid sitting
down with me and talking openly about these issues. They said
things behind my back, called Ambedkar names. My blood
would begin to boil at such betrayals.

In the end I began to boycott these religious celebrations. I
searched for theater people who were keen to work for change. We
staged many Dalit plays. One was *Mumbai Nagri* by Daya Pawar.

A convocation of Nagpur University was held in Chandrapur.
Meghdoot Natya Sanstha staged a play at the convocation. Many
intellectuals, writers, and professors commented positively about
the production.

A letter came from the village. Ma was ill. Chanda and I went to
the village and stayed a week. Ma was getting better but she had
become as thin as a reed. I was very shaken, looking at her condition. Something, somewhere was slipping away from my grasp and
scattering like sand.

Ma passed away a week after our return to Chandrapur. But I
got the news after two months. My nephew Devendra sent me a
postcard that took two months to reach me. I could not control
myself when I read the postcard. My inability to participate in her
last journey pricked my heart like a thorn. This pain continues to
rankle even now. I might have been able to reach home in time had
Pitaji sent me a telegram. But there was no point in recrimina-

tions. Pitaji's health had also began to decline after Ma's death. I was constantly besieged by a fear that Pitaji might pass away just like Ma, without my being present. That's what happened. I went to see him and he died the day I left. I was probably on the train when he died. I got a letter many days after my return to Chandrapur.

I was not granted the privilege to carry Ma's and Pitaji's biers. He whom they had struggled so hard to make something of had become so distanced from them. It is a grief that I hide deep inside my heart.

R. Kamal was in Kanpur. He brought out a magazine called *Nirnayak Bhim*. He published my writings in almost every issue. I invited him to Chandrapur for a function. He was a vibrant, electrifying personality, and he was spreading Ambedkar's message in the Hindi-speaking regions. *Nirnayak Bhim* had made its presence felt among the Hindi Dalit magazines. It had provided an outlet for Dalit writers. After returning from his tour of Maharashtra, he had written that the Dalit consciousness in Hindi provinces had not seen a similar awakening, that we would need to work steadily to achieve our goals. Similarly, Mohandas Naimishray, the poet, writer, and journalist, also came to Chandrapur at our invitation, and we arranged events for him at many places. At the time Naimishray was writing as a freelancer.

My activities were no longer confined to Maharashtra. I attended many functions in Madhya Pradesh to discuss Dalit problems. The more active I became in the Dalit movement, the more suspicious people around me became, as though I was working to destroy their domination. Most of these suspicious people were *savarnas*. I began to notice the effects of this surveillance among my fellow employees too.

The distant rural areas of Chandrapur district were showing no signs of modern civilization and development. The women did not wear any clothes on the upper portion of their bodies. Their diet was meager. Their forest-based agriculture produced only *jowar* and low-quality rice.[5] The harvest depended entirely on rainfall. The India that I encountered during my travels in these villages was dirt poor and drowning in superstitions. In one such village a tantric had made a sacrificial offering of a child to increase the yield in his field.[6] Five or six of us went to that village. The Marathi daily *Lokmat* drew the attention of the whole nation to this incident. The police became alert and arrested many villagers along with the tantric. Incidents like these impelled me to write. I believed that it was more meaningful to write about the travails of the ordinary people than to sing about the glories of the past.

In January 1984 an incident that took place in Malkapur in the Amravati district that epitomized the narrow-mindedness of these parts. A Marathi textbook meant for class seven included a lesson on Ambedkar. All the students ripped out the lesson on the orders of a Brahmin teacher. The class included some Mahar students, and they felt that ripping out the lesson was wrong. Those students quietly picked up the torn pages from the rubbish and took them home to show them to their families. The news spread. Protests began. Someone sent a detailed account along with the torn pages to *Lokmat*'s Nagpur bureau. *Lokmat* published the story and photographs of the torn pages. Rallies and protest meetings began all over Vidarbha as soon as the story broke.[7] This incident became a symbol of Dalit oppression.

Thousands upon thousands of people came to a huge rally staged at Bhadravati. I too addressed the rally. Most speakers spoke in Marathi. I spoke in Hindi. This was a new experience for me. The crowd was simmering with anger. At that moment I experienced my belonging to the Dalit movement intensely. I wrote a

---

5. *Jowar* is a coarse grain, like millet.

6. A tantric is someone who knows traditional black magic and casts spells, practicing a debased form of the ancient art of tantra.

7. Vidarbha is the eastern region of Maharashtra, and Malkapur is a small town in that region.

poem entitled "Vidrup Chehra" (Crooked Face), and many magazines and newspapers published it.

The movement was gathering force by the day. In many places
savarnas threw stones at Dalit marchers and rallies. The police
were indifferent. The board of education took no disciplinary
action against the teacher [who had told the students to tear the
Ambedkar chapter from their books]. While Dalits called impassioned meetings in many places, the administration was trying to
suppress the whole thing. This whole episode affected me deeply.
Now I was spending most of my time in Dalit *bastis*.

Near the ordnance factory was a village called Sumthana,
which I have mentioned earlier. In the Bhadravati district we started many programs in the Dalit *bastis*. We opened many schools.
Umesh Meshram ran a school and a library at Bhadravati. It
stocked plenty of books on Ambedkar and Buddhism, and
Meshram often invited me to come and give a talk.

Bhadravati had an ancient Buddhist cave where celebrations
were held on Buddha Purnima.[8] Umesh Meshram and his group
had organized the Buddhist Writers Conference, where I had the
opportunity to meet many Marathi Dalit writers. Here I came in
close contact with Jyoti Langevar, Bhimsen Dete, Loknath
Yashwant, Bhagwan Thag, and a few others.

Although I had a correspondence going with the Dalit writer
Dr. Gangadhar Pantavne, I had never had the occasion to meet
him. One day, all of a sudden, Loknath Yashvant sent word to me
that Pantavne Guruji—most people addressed him that way—
was coming to participate in the Anand Mela, held at Baba Amte's
ashram. I attended this fair almost every year. Baba Amte's ashram
was in Varora; it treated leprosy patients and helped them to
become self-reliant. Writers, intellectuals, and artists from all over
Maharashtra came to the ashram to attend the Anand Mela. The
fair lasted two days. There I met P. L. Deshpande, Marathi's

---

8. Buddha Purnima is Buddha's birth anniversary. Calculated according to the lunar
calendar, it always falls on a full moon, or Purnima, in May.

famous dramaturge, satirist, and novelist. There I had the great fortune to hear singers like Vasantrao Deshpande, Bhimsen Joshi, and Kishori Amonkar.

Loknath Yashvant introduced me to Guruji. He met me with great openness. Guruji was devoid of pretensions of any sort. His Hindi had a Marathi accent. He spoke very slowly, but his words seemed imbued with great feeling. For many days afterward I was intoxicated by this short meeting. Pantavne Guruji translated my poems into Marathi. Truly, for an unknown poet like me, this was a great honor. *Asmitadarsh* magazine created an outlet for Marathi Dalit literature, encouraging new writers. Ganagadhar Pantavne's contribution as editor of *Asmitadarsh* is an important milestone in the development of Dalit literature.

Kureishi and I met at a poetry reading. He was a subinspector for the Maharashtra police. Gregarious and a connoisseur of literature, Kureishi lived in Nagpur. He had joined the police force because he needed a job, not out of preference, and it took him quite a while to get into the role of a policeman. He was in charge of the police station at the ordnance factory. He lived in a bungalow on the DSC Line [the neighborhood where the police lived], very close to the police station. He and I became intimate friends after only a couple of meetings.

Whenever Kureishi had to go on night duty or on a short trip out of town, he would leave his wife at my place. She was a beautiful woman. Kureishi didn't like leaving her alone in the DSC Line. He often brought her to my house even at 2, 2:30 at night. Chanda and Mrs. Kureishi got on very well. The Kureishis had twin sons who were really adorable. Chanda called them Ram and Shyam, the names of Hindu gods, and Kureishi, a Muslim, also started calling them by these names. The kids became very attached to us.

The new commandant of the DSC had just arrived, and he was allotted the bungalow next to Kureishi's. He was from Muzaffarnagar district. When Kureishi found this out, he mentioned it to me, and said, "He is from your district. Why don't you drop by this evening and I will introduce you to him?"

I wasn't too keen on meeting him, and Kureishi sensed my hesitation. He became a bit upset and said, "You are a very strange man. You find a person from your own area in this strange land and yet you don't seem happy."

I said, "What is the point? The moment I meet him, he will

ask about my caste. The moment he finds out my caste, he will feel nauseous."

Kureishi said with bitterness, "Valmiki, when are you going to come out of that shell of yours?"

That day a heated argument got going between us. Finally, we decided that I would go and meet him just to see if I was right. Kureishi held that army people didn't pay attention to things like caste. "You suspect everybody because you have developed a complex," he stated.

The next day I went to Kureishi's bungalow along with Chanda. Mrs. Kureishi's *biryani* was as fantastic as usual. Leaving Chanda at Kureishi's place, Kureishi and I went over to the commandant's bungalow. We found him right on the veranda. Kureishi introduced us. He gave my name as Omprakash, "forgetting" the Valmiki.

Commandant Sahib received me with great warmth. He was delighted when he heard that I was from Barla. Before we even sat down, he asked, "Barla is a Tyagi village. Which caste are you from?" I looked at Kureishi, whose face had changed color. He had asked the question conversationally. The moment I said that my caste was Chuhra, the commandant became uneasy. Suddenly all conversation stopped, as though we had nothing left to talk about. This was a new experience for Kureishi.

I said to Kureishi, "Shall we leave now, or is there anything else?" Kureishi's mood had been spoiled. He got up. "Accha, Commandant Sahib, we will be off now." Kureishi and I left the bungalow.

The next day the commandant had tried to reason with Kureishi, "Kureishi Sahib, he is considered a low caste in our district. He and his like are not allowed to cross the threshold, and here you are socializing with him, even dining with him." Kureishi had put a full stop to his sermon right there. After that day he even stopped saying hello to the commandant. Kureishi and I grew even closer.

Chandrapur was a backward district of Maharashtra, its boundaries touching Andhra Pradesh and Madhya Pradesh. It saw rapid
industrialization in the 1980s. Its local coal deposits are among the
largest in the country. Rapid industrialization also led to an
increase in crime. *Dacoits*, or gang members who rob and murder,
were striking every day, and kidnapping was becoming quite common. The police were on the alert. Sharad Pawar, the chief minister, was under political pressure to do something, so the reserve
force also was brought in to help the local police.

Chanda had gone to Dehra Dun, and I was alone at home. At
10 P.M. I heard a police jeep stop outside. When I looked out the
window, I saw Kureishi was getting out of the vehicle. I opened
the door and Kureishi said, "Come. Let us take you out on the
night beat."

I asked, "Where?"

"Oh, just come along," he said impatiently. In the jeep were a
Mr. Verma, an inspector of the provincial police, and four or five
constables. Kureishi introduced me to Mr. Verma on the way. He
was in charge of the special Dacoity Eradication Force. Tonight he
was out on [*dacoit*] patrol duty. I was a bit worried. What new
trouble was Kureishi getting me into today? But Inspector Verma's
easy manners inspired courage in me, and I prepared myself men-
tally for a pleasant outing.

After Colony Checkpost the jeep turned toward the
Bhadravati gas pump. We filled up with gas and then came out on
the national highway. The jeep was now going really fast. We had-
n't gone even four or five kilometers when we heard the siren of the
car of the superintendent of police, coming from the Varora side.
All the people in our jeep became apprehensive. The superintendent's car stopped beside the jeep. We all got out and stood in line.
Looking at my civilian clothes, the superintendent asked Kureishi,
"Who is that in the jeep?"

Kureishi replied promptly, "Sir! We are taking him to Varora
for interrogation."

I have no idea what Kureishi's comment said to the superin-

tendent, but my heartbeat went up. The moment the superintendent's car drove off, everyone quickly got into the jeep. We all
breathed a sigh of relief. I was still scared. I asked Kureishi, "What
sort of a mess are you getting me into?"

Kureishi laughed out aloud. Inspector Verma, taking my hand
in both of his, assured me, "You are our guest tonight. Don't worry
about anything."

The jeep came to a sudden halt at some place. They all got out
and stood around. Kureishi and Verma were standing together,
away. I kept sitting in the jeep. They were stopping trucks and cars
and interrogating people. One truck coming from Andhra Pradesh
was loaded with red chili pepper. The police ordered the driver
and the cleaner off the truck and demanded that they empty it out
for checking. The truck driver knew what this demand implied.

After much to-ing and fro-ing, the driver stuffed some rupees
into the hand of a policeman and the drama suddenly came to an
end. They repeated the same ploy with eight or ten trucks. I
looked at this game from inside the jeep. I had had many arguments with Kureishi about this sort of police corruption. He had
his point—if he didn't participate in such acts, his superiors would
consider him a fink. Because he had demonstrated scruples about
not taking bribes earlier in his career, he had already received a
negative performance review. In the end he was forced to become
part of the system. I did not have an instrument with which I
could measure the truth of his arguments. One time I said,
"Kureishi, this is a great way to hide your crimes. Blame everything
on your superiors. I am sure that your superiors must do the same
and blame their subordinates for everything."

We reached Vani at 12:30 at night. A fair was going on, and
as soon as the jeep stopped at the fairground, the policemen dis-
persed. Kureishi and Verma sat down on chairs that were lying
in front of a tea stall. The tea stall owner treated them royally.
After sitting there for some time, waiting for the policemen to
return, Inspector Verma asked Kureishi, "Where the hell have
they gone to die?"

Kureishi replied angrily, "Where else? They have gone to frolic with their mothers and sisters."

The fair attracted a lot of prostitutes. The police turned a blind eye toward them, and it was quite possible that the police were collecting kickbacks from these women. Just thinking about it left a bitter taste in my mouth. At such times I felt as though Kureishi had sprouted horns. He seemed to have a split personality. Sometimes I felt that if Kureishi had not joined the police, he might have been a good poet.

The Dacoity Eradication Force left the fair around 2 A.M. After some nominal checking in a village or two, we were back on the tarred road. Back at Varora police station, Kureishi and Verma went inside to report on the night's work, leaving me alone in the jeep.

I stretched out on the backseat and fell asleep. Kureishi woke me up. "Would you like a cup of tea?" he asked. A policeman stood with a cup of tea in his hand. The sip of tea woke me up at least momentarily. Kureishi dropped me off at my quarters at 5 A.M. and returned to the police lines. My eyes were heavy with sleep, and I fell asleep the moment I hit the bed.

It was quite late in the day when I awoke. Because it was Sunday, I had no reason to rush. I made myself a cup of tea, and as I was turning the pages of the newspaper, a headline caught my attention. Another attack by the *dacoits* had occurred in some village. I recalled anew the activities of the previous night. The expedition of the Dacoity Eradication Force was engraved on my memory.

Kureishi came round again at about 2:30 P.M. The same people were with him. The superintendent had asked him to report to his office, which was in the city, thirty kilometers away from the colony. Kureishi had come to take me along. I refused, but he was insistent, and I finally agreed to go with him.

Just past Ghorpeth we saw a fifteen- or sixteen-year-old boy on foot with a bag slung on his shoulder. Kureishi ordered the driver to stop and called the boy over. The boy was visibly frightened on seeing the police jeep. Kureishi asked him sternly, "Where are you going?"

"To my village." The boy sounded frightened.

"Which village?" Kureishi demanded.

"Near Vani," the boy replied haltingly.

"Near Vani, eh? How can you walk that distance?" The police-man inside Kureishi's split personality was beginning to raise his head.

"Yes, Sahib . . . I don't have money for the bus fare." The boy's voice was choked.

Kureishi fired the next question. "Where are you coming from?"

The boy seemed very shaky. He was talking about some hotel in Chandrapur. He used to work there. The hotel owner had not given him leave or his outstanding pay for the past four months. The boy did not have the money to go from Chandrapur to Vani by bus. He had heard that his mother was ill, and he was walking to his village to see her.

Kureishi administered three or four slaps during this inter-rogation.

"You are lying. Come on, tell me exactly what you are up to."

"Sahib, I swear in God's name. I am telling the truth." The boy had begun to speak in Marathi as soon as he was slapped.

My eyes were popping out of their sockets as I watched Kureishi. I found his behavior bizarre, and I said, "Kureishi, in your eyes this boy may be a liar, a thief, or a *dacoit* or god knows what. But what is true is that he has no money in his pocket—and still you are assaulting him. The hotel owner who didn't pay him his salary, you can't even raise a finger at him. Can you policemen find a law to help the boy? To help him get the salary that is owed him? Or does your Penal Code consist only of beating him up?"

This interference surprised Kureishi for a few seconds. The boy also felt a bit braver. He grabbed Kureishi's feet and said, "Sahib, I am telling the truth, you go to the hotel and see for yourself."[1]

---

1. Touching a person's feet is a gesture of respect from a social subordinate or from a younger person.

Kureishi ordered him into the jeep. He had given the name of a hotel near the Chandrapur railway bridge. The jeep stopped right in front of the hotel. The hotel owner looked abashed when he saw the servant with the police. Kureishi read the man's reaction. His voice dripping with authority, Kureishi asked, "This boy works in your hotel?"

"Ji . . . Sahib . . . What has he done?" The owner tried to pretend that he knew nothing.

Kureishi fired off another question, "Why haven't you given him his pay?"

"I will give it right away, Sahib . . . He didn't report to work today." The hotel owner was opening his drawer.

"How many months since you paid him?" Kureishi asked.

"Sahib, business is down these days," the hotel owner bleated.

The servant felt a little empowered and he said to Kureishi, "Sahib, he hasn't given me a single paisa in four months."

The hotel owner put four months' salary in the boy's hand. The boy's face was streaked with joy. Kureishi smiled at me. I said, "Kureishi, you have added at least one good deed to your ledger."

The boy showed his gratitude by once again touching Kureishi's feet.

Ballarpur Paper Mills sponsored a drama competition every year. This competition for Hindi and Marathi plays was important not only for the theater people but also for the audience in the Ballarpur area. Meghdoot Natya Sanstha had made a name for itself in this competition by staging plays like *Aadhe Adhure*, *Himalaya ki Chhaya*, *Sinhasan Khali Hai*, and *Paisa Bolta Hai*. We won many prizes. I was awarded the best actor and the best director prize several times. Chanda won the best actress prize for her central roles in *Himalaya ki Chhaya* and *Aadhe Adhure*. This competition brought me into contact with friends and guides like Dr. Hira Lal Verma and Kishan Sharma. Hira Lal

Verma was a good playwright. His play *Mercy Killing* had been well received.

Kishan Sharma was a senior announcer in Akashvani's Nagpur Vividh Bharati Centre and a popular stage actor. He introduced me to people in Akashvani. He loved me like an elder brother. Chanda respected him greatly. Kishan Sharmaji has played a large role in helping me to develop my potential. He is a great artist and a great human being who has the capacity to respond to others with tremendous sensitivity.

I met Dr. Hanumant Naidu during a poetry reading at the ordnance factory. I felt drawn to him in our very first meeting. He was the head of the Hindi department at Nagpur University. Besides composing excellent *ghazals* [lyric love poems in Urdu], he also wrote a satirical column for *Navbharat*. Whenever I had the opportunity to visit Nagpur, I went to his house without fail. He was my mentor, bringing my weaknesses to my attention. He polished my language. And he brought me into contact with Vijay Vyas and Rajjan Trivedi. Vijay Vyas was editing a literary column for *Navbharat*, which was an important outlet for emerging writers. Vijay Vyas published my poems in this column, along with his critical commentary.

At Naidu's house I met the famous poet and songwriter Virendra Mishra. All the well-known writers and poets of Nagpur used to gather at Naidu's place. Although Naidu did not comment openly about my Dalit-related writings, he felt that untouchability was no longer a relevant topic. Many a time I suspected that we had ideological disagreements, but his affection made me push these aside.

The time that I spent with Bhadant Anand Kausalyayan is one of the most precious keepsakes of my life. Kausalyayanji spent a long time with Ambedkar and Rahul Sankrityayan. I had become familiar with Rahulji's work very early on. Whereas *Manav Samaj* had made me conversant with the process of human evolution, *Vaigyanic Bhautikvad* had erased the existence of God from my mind. *Volga se Ganga* had given rise to a new consciousness in me.

The lies that the textbooks had been injecting in my veins in the name of cultural heritage were shattered by *Volga se Ganga*.

I gave copies of *Volga se Ganga* and *Manav Samaj* to a friend of mine who was proud of India's past glory. Reading these books shook him up. An intellectual ferment began inside him. He wasn't capable, however, of freeing himself from the vise of the *samskaras*.[2] He would become unsettled the moment he heard anyone mention Rahul Sankrityayan's name.

I read many books on Buddhism that Rahulji had translated, *Anguttar Nikai*, *Majham Nikai*, *Sanyukt Nikai*, *Suttpitik*, *Dirgh Nikai*, *Buddha Darshan*, and so on. These books inspired a new consciousness in me. I enjoyed listening to Kausalyayanji reminiscing about Rahulji. I have always regretted that I did not get to meet Rahulji. His books are as indispensable to me as staying alive. Books like *Darshan Digdarshan*, *Tibet ki Yatrayen*, and *Cheen Yatra* brought the world to my door. Kausalyayanji knew details of Rahul Sankrityayan's life that I have not come across anywhere else.

Along with poetry and drama, I was also beginning to turn to the short story form. I had always been a reader of short stories, and I began to write them myself around 1978–79. I submitted "Jungal ki Rani," a story based on *adivasi* [indigenous] life, to *Sarika*. Avadhnarayan Mudgal was the editor of *Sarika* at that time. Ramesh Batra and Suresh Uniyal were also at *Sarika*. I received a letter of acceptance. *Sarika* was the center of literary activities in Hindi at that time. All new writers wanted to be published in *Sarika*. I jumped with joy when I got the acceptance letter.

Sarika held on to that story for many years. In the meanwhile, whenever I visited the city, I went to *Sarika*'s office and reminded the editors of my short story and would receive a reassurance from Suresh Uniyal each time. Subhash Pant was a friend of Suresh Uniyal's, and I asked Subhash Pant to talk to him. I have no idea whether he did so, but Suresh Uniyal asked me to send them a new copy, which I did.

---

2. Hindu rites and rituals that are a part of the upper-caste Hindu's life.

Both copies of the short story came back to me in 1990 with a
typed letter that said that we haven't been able to publish your
story thus far, but please send it back if you are willing to wait
longer. That is, after making me wait for ten full years, they wanted me to wait longer. What kind of a joke is this? The literary
establishment crushes newly sprouted talents. *Sarika* closed down.
Who knows how many writers like me were discouraged by the
Sarika editorial board? Anyway, despite publishing a deluge of special issues, they couldn't save their own hide, so how were they
going to save us newcomers? Although the treatment meted out to
me wasn't unusual in literary circles, I kept feeling that the editors
and established writers had conspired to prevent new writers from
emerging. I am grateful to *Hans*, which published my short stories.
The solicitousness with which Rajendra Yadav published my work
gave me a new life, although the ones who wanted me dead left
nothing to chance.

Our department at the ordnance factory started a new project
in Dehra Dun. When they asked for applications, I submitted one
too, and my application was approved in April 1985. But the general manager stalled it. The joint general manager, Shri Goyal, was
a good friend of mine. He loved *shairi*.[3] I found out what was happening through him. Armed with this information, I went to see
the general manager, Shri S. S. Natarajan. He didn't want to lose
me, but when I told him how keen I was to go to Dehra Dun, he
agreed to let me go.

On June 22, 1985, I transferred from the ordnance factory in
Chandrapur to the ordnance factory in Dehra Dun. I had been in
Chandrapur for almost thirteen years. When I was leaving
Chandrapur, I felt as though I was leaving home. Chandrapur gave
me so much.

Chanda also did not like leaving Chandrapur. She had
become so much a part of the community there that she was find-

---

3. *Shairi* are Urdu poems, often recited in formal gatherings of poets either by the
composer or by a well-known poet.

ing it very hard to leave behind. Salig Singh Sapkale's wife, Vandana, and their children were like our family. Manni would call me Daddy and Chanda Ai, or Mother in Marathi. Her own mother she called by her first name. Leaving them behind was difficult for Chanda. We didn't sleep at all that night. Vandana, Salig, and Manni sat up with us. We had to leave early in the morning. That morning was unbelievably painful.

We left for Dehra Dun by the G. T. Express, and all those people with whom we had shared our joys and sorrows remained behind. To this day the fragrance of Maharashtra's soil is fresh in my nostrils.

The last part of my name, which is also called the surname, has landed me in a lot of dire situations because it is also a marker of caste. When these situations affect my relations with others, I begin to wonder if I should get rid of it. Despite many disasters, I have not been able to let go of it. In fact, it has begun to sound even more a part of me.

A well-known Marathi Dalit poet, Loknath Yashwant, finds my surname attractive. Many friends consider my surname significant. A commonplace name like "Omprakash" has become distinctive by the addition of "Valmiki," they believe. In school and in college my classmates and teachers made many pejorative comments about this surname. I was often the butt of their jokes. But some found it the signifier of a courageous act. They argued that when an untouchable uses his caste name as his surname with a feeling of self-assertion, he is being very brave. One gentleman has ripped this argument to pieces: "What is so brave about that? . . . After all he is a Chuhra. His surname spares us the hassle of asking what his caste is."

Some people think that it is a foolish move, especially at a time when honor and insult are doled out on the basis of caste. They believe that as soon as people find out about my surname, their behavior changes. Those who hold this opinion are either the educated among my caste or members of my own family and other relatives. Some of them are so-called Dalit writers. Many officials and scholars try to keep me at a distance. Soon after I finished my training at the Ordnance Factory Training Institute in Khamaria, Jabalpur, I filled out an application for a competitive examination, which had to be submitted to the trainer in charge, Mr. Gupta. He belonged to some village near Meerut, and he was well aware of the meaning of the surname Valmiki. He turned the pages of my application many times, as though he could not believe his eyes. Seeing Barla, Muzaffarnagar, as my permanent address, his anger and surprise had burst out together: "Abey, *sohare*, he has got this far!"[4]

I felt that his way of speaking to me was unjust. When I protested, he got even more enraged and obnoxious. "You! . . . You will teach me manners?" he bellowed. His behavior made me very angry. A classmate standing beside me was a witness to this outrage. He tried to calm me down. After we left Gupta's office, he said, "You are in training right now. These people want you to take a wrong step so that they can throw you out of the institute. Learn to recognize their traps."

This incident has buried itself deep in my heart like a splinter. After completing the training and getting selected in the competition, I went for further training at the Ordnance Factory Training Institute in Ambernath, Bombay, where I had to do a two-year course. This course became my entry to a regular job. If I had gotten into a fight that day with Gupta, a fight that almost happened, it would have destroyed my future. How much have I had to endure to get this far!

During my stay in Maharashtra some people mistook me for a Brahmin because of my Valmiki surname. One Deshpande in Ambernath made this assumption. He would often invite me to his home. One day something he said in conversation made me realize that he thought that I was a Brahmin like he was.

---

4. *Shohare* means father-in-law, used as abuse.

When I immediately let the secret out, he became a bit discon-
certed. Suddenly, a yawning gap appeared between us. We were
never able to go back to our easy friendship after that.

Not only outsiders but my own family began to be bothered
by my surname. Pitaji, of course, was an exception. Although he
was illiterate, he could think differently from the others. He was
absolutely honest and self-reliant. He used to call himself
Sharbhang, an epithet whose meaning escapes me to this day. He
didn't have an iota of an inferiority complex. He had a stubborn
temperament, which was reflected in everything about him,
whether his manner of speaking or his gait.

He didn't know for the longest time that I used Valmiki as my
last name. He was pleased when he found out. His eyes gleamed
with pleasure, a gleam that is still fresh in my memory.

My wife, Chanda, has never managed to get used to this surname of mine. Nor does she use it herself. This name is an item on
her list of my shortcomings, and once in a while she comments on
it. She prefers using our family's *gotra* name, "Khairwal."[5]

I have talked about the theater group Meghdoot Natya
Sanstha. Chanda and I ran it for ten years, right up to the day of
our transfer. Both of us were active in the theater during those
days. We staged many plays together. In publicity materials
Chanda would use Khairwal as her last name, and she would pressure me to use it too. When I tried to avoid the issue, she came
back with arguments that made me accept defeat. Once I almost
gave in, thinking that changing my surname was better than this
daily squabbling. But I came back to my old surname with an even
greater determination.

Even today, when family members are discussing this surname, Chanda says adamantly, "If we had had a child, I would definitely have made you change your surname." When I hear her say

5. *Gotra* refers to the name of a large kinship group of many families within a caste
who supposedly share a common ancestor; the name must be given when any ritual
is performed.

that, I feel as though my wife is talking about changing our residence or clothes. Such comments do torment me. I become unsettled when I hear them.

I have a friend named Dinesh Manav who is in Rampur these days. Earlier, he used to live in Allahabad. He was an active journalist and started a magazine called *Mahodika*. The magazine, which would close after just one issue, carried a poem and an article of mine. The byline said only "Omprakash," that is, my surname had been excised. An editor's note said that the magazine would not publish surnames that denoted caste. This is how he was going to eradicate casteism.

The Dalits who have become educated face a terrible crisis—the crisis of identity—and they are trying to find an easy and instantaneous way to get out of this crisis. They have started to use their family *gotra* as their surname after just a little bit of fine-tuning. For instance, Chinaliye has become Chandril or Chanchal, and Saude has been changed to Saudai or Sood. One gentleman has converted Parchha to Partha. My mother's family's *gotra* is Kesle, which some people have changed to Keswal. They find that the easy way out. Behind all such acts is the anguish of identity crisis, which has come about as a reaction to the blatant inhumanity of casteism. Dalits want to join the mainstream of society after getting an education, but the *savarnas* prevent them from doing so. They discriminate against Dalits. They think of them as inferior beings. They cast doubts on their intelligence, their ability, their performance. They use all kinds of nefarious means to attack Dalits. Only he whose skin has suffered the knife wounds of this terrorizing can recognize this pain. These knife wounds haven't just injured the skin but also have scarred the inner being. In these times of dire danger to our existence, when a man like me comes around with his caste-marker surname, all those people who want to hide their caste become wary. They feel that someone is letting out their secret. They find it easier to run away from the problem. But the truth is that change won't come about through running away. It will come about through struggle and engagement.

Mohandas Naimishray was living in Arya Nagar, New Delhi, then. I would stay at his place whenever I visited Delhi. Chanda was being treated at the All India Institute of Medical Sciences (AIIMS), and we had had to come all the way from Chandrapur. Naimishrayji's wife, Shakuntalaji, helped us way beyond what a close relative would have done. She took leave from work to make the rounds of hospitals and doctors' clinics. She stood for hours without food or water on the verandas of AIIMS, waiting for our number to be called.

Naimishrayji took me to meet an editor friend of his. Naimishrayji had worked in the editorial division of this friend's magazine for some time. The magazine's office was located in the editor's home. As we were climbing the stairs to the house, Naimishrayji said, "How about introducing you just as 'Omprakash'"?

I felt a jolt as I heard him. I asked, "Why?"

"He does not know too much about me . . . He seems to be a good man . . . Respects me a lot . . . Still . . ." Naimishrayji tried to clarify.

At first I felt like turning back, but running away was not going to solve the problem. I walked on behind Naimishrayji. Jain Sahib was sitting in the chair facing the door. Before Naimishrayji could formally introduce me, I went forward and introduced myself. He met us with great warmth. His comments or behavior did not suggest that he was negatively affected by my surname.

The writers, intellectuals, and activists in the Dalit movement have to struggle constantly with their inner conflicts. There is so much fear lurking in the dark recesses of the heart that prevents us from leading normal lives. My niece Seema was studying for her bachelor's degree. Dr. Kusum Chaturvedi, a writer of fiction, was the head of the Hindi department. One day I happened to mention to her that my niece was a student of hers. The next day, when Chaturvedi went to the class, she asked Seema, "Do you know Omprakash Valmiki?" Seema looked around the class and denied that she knew me. In the evening she told me the whole story and tried to justify herself. "If I had acknowledged in front of everybody that you are my uncle, then my classmates would know that I am a Valmiki. You may be able to face it. I can't. What is the point of going around with the drum of caste tied around your neck?" Seema's argument stood before me like a distorted portrait of the entire social order. Seema and Chanda had joined forces against my surname.

When I came to Dehra Dun after being transferred from Chandrapur, I faced the problem of finding a house. After wandering around for a whole month, I was able to rent a two-room house from Dr. Sindhwani in Karanpur. We had to fit all our belongings into two small rooms. The problem was not that Dehra Dun had a shortage of rental accommodations or that I was not able to pay the rent. The moment the landlords heard my last name, they either refused me point-blank or made some excuse or the other.

Bhola Ram Khare lived a block away from Dr. Sindhwani's house. I had known his wife, Rameshwari, for a long time. They were also Valmiki but used Khare as their surname. Through them I had managed to find somewhere to live. Their daughter Manju worked in a bank. She would come to visit Chanda regularly in the evenings or on weekends. They became *nanad-bhabhi*. I too became subsumed in their establishment of this relationship. Manju was getting married. I took on the responsibility of making all the arrangements, doing my best to fulfill the obligations of being an elder brother. I took leave from work to make sure that everything was taken care of. Chanda assumed the responsibility for things inside the household. Everything was moving along smoothly.

When Manju's wedding invitations arrived from the printer, they caused an incident. In the list of family members and friends my name was missing. I decided to overlook the omission, but my wife was troubled by it. She went ahead and asked Manju to explain why my name was left out. Manju tried to make some excuse, but Chanda inherited a stubborn temperament. She insisted on the truth and forced Manju to come out with it.

"Bhabhi, no one here knows that we are Valmiki. They all think we are Khare. Printing Bhaiya's name would have let the secret out . . .," Manju said, her voice cracking.

This gave Chanda yet another occasion to fulminate against my surname. A similar incident occurred with another relative. The wedding cards of Chanda's niece also had everybody's name except mine.

All this does not mean that my relations with these relatives are not close. They are all very dear to me. But my surname carries the threat of their being found out. The stings that this surname has made me endure are hard to describe. Why talk about the others when my own family and friends have caused me unspeakable anguish? It is easy to battle against the outsiders; the most arduous battle has to be fought against one's own.

Dr. Sukhvir Singh was an associate professor at Delhi University's Shivaji College. A Hindi scholar, critic, and poet, he was also unhappy with my surname. Once I spent a night at his house in Vishwas Nagar, Shahdara. I had to speak to Shrikrishnaji of Parag Publications about my novel *Kali Ret*, and Dr. Sukhvir Singhji accompanied me. Shrikrishnaji agreed to publish the novel. (The novel remains unpublished but for reasons other than my name.)

That night I had a long discussion with Sukhvir Singh about the surname Valmiki. He had deleted Valmiki from my name and replaced it with Khairwal. I had written a review of his recently published book, *Suryansh*, and he had taken the review to the office of *Aajkal*, a journal. When a member of the editorial board expressed surprise that Omprakash was using Khairwal as a surname, Sukhvir Singh had said, "From now on we won't call him Valmiki but Khairwal." He had crossed out Valmiki with his own hand and replaced it with Khairwal. That review was published in *Aajkal* under the name of Omprakash Khairwal.

Sukhvir Singh was also afraid of having his identity revealed. That's why he didn't want to be associated with my surname. Harikishan Santoshi had a similar problem. He has mocked this surname of mine many times. He has a friend named Sardar Gyan Singh who comes from Khekhra village near Meerut. He knows me through my Dalit writings. He is impressed by my poems and short stories. He often writes long letters to me, and while these contain encouraging comments on my writing, he also tries to advise me that I am a well-educated fool. He regards me as no better than an illiterate person because of my holding onto my surname. He contends that I am knowingly immersed in the "Brahminist" swamp, that I should give up Valmiki as a surname. He has often tried to reason with me by giving the example of Harikishan Santoshiji and his wife.

I get a lot of invitations from organizations of sanitation employees, inviting me to meetings, panels, and conventions. Once when I mentioned this to Harikishan Santoshiji, he smiled and said, "That's what will happen if you keep using Valmiki. You will be seen as a sanitation employee."

Some of the letters that I get from my readers are from young Valmikis, who want to add Valmiki to their names. Mahendra Bainiwal, who is an emerging poet, has also expressed a desire to use Valmiki as a surname. We had a long correspondence on the matter. He used Valmiki for some time but later changed to Bainiwal.

Not long ago I was invited to give a lecture on Buddhist literature and philosophy at a conference. Two or three scholars spoke before me. As soon as I got to the mike, a member of the audience shouted, "How can a Valmiki be allowed to speak on Buddhist literature and philosophy? Aren't you ashamed?"

His comment poisoned the atmosphere. The organizers tried to stop him, but he wasn't willing to listen to my arguments. When I began speaking on the pervasive spread of casteism in Hindu society, he quieted down a bit. The organizers were unhappy about this incident, but for me it was an educational experience. I feel that the problem is far-reaching and its proposed solutions most-

ly superficial. There has been no dialogue on the internal contradictions.[6]

During a meeting with Dr. Dharmvir [a scholar], we talked
about the negativity that my surname generates. He had said,
"Don't remove it. It has become your badge of identity."

A conference of Dalit writers from five states, Delhi, Punjab,
Haryana, Himachal, and Uttar Pradesh, was held at Chandigarh.
I was to speak during the last session of the two-day conference.
Dalip Singh, an advocate, spoke after me. He is a former legislator
and a good speaker. He made positive comments on my surname,
giving me much encouragement. He also commented on my
poems and short stories. His remarks raised certain issues that led
to a lot of heated discussion in the last session. The Valmiki surname had shown its effect here as well.

All the writers stayed at Kisan Bhavan. I was staying with my
friend Ram Singhji at his place in sector 47. His wife, Induji, is a
woman of literary sensibility. She is fond of reading and thinking
about books. I told her about the discussion at my session.
Although she had never been able to say it openly before, that day
she said haltingly, "This Valmiki surname isn't appropriate." We
did not discuss the issue in detail that day. Nor was there a possibility of openly discussing it.

The next day they dropped me off at the bus terminal. In the
sector 47 bus terminal, drivers and conductors were sitting on the
benches. Most of them were Sikhs, and they were arguing animatedly: "Whatever you say, a Chuhra will remain a Chuhra. Howsoever
high an officer he may become, he cannot change his caste."

Induji looked at me. Her eyes seemed to ask a question,
"What do you think, O writer? Can you still defend your surname?" She spoke after a short silence. "This surname of yours will
drastically blemish your prestige one day." Her daughter, Sonia,

---

6. The internal contradiction is that Buddhism was an anticaste movement and the
Buddha said that there was no basis for untouchability, yet Valmiki is using a surname that declares his caste; he is suggesting that just removing surnames does not
eliminate caste, that it is also an issue in Buddhism. See also the introduction.

who was standing beside her, spoke up. "Uncle, I will write Valmiki after my name." Induji's son, Sahil, was finding it hard to understand this conversation. Induji was taken aback by her daughter's remark. Full of apprehension for the future, she stood silently, her gaze fixed on the bus drivers and the conductors.

At my office many of my colleagues and subordinates undervalue my worth because of this surname. In the early days I used to get angry. In my rage I would clash with people. It is not that I don't protest now. However, my approach is different today. Now I can take it with the attitude that I am contending with a a societal disease. When caste is the basis of respect and merit, important for social superiority, this battle cannot be won in a day. We need an ongoing struggle and a consciousness of struggle, a consciousness that brings revolutionary change both in the outside world and in our hearts, a consciousness that leads the process of social change.

This surname is now an indispensable part of my name. "Omprakash" has no identity without it. *Identity* and *recognition*— the two words say a lot by themselves. Ambedkar was born in a Dalit family. But Ambedkar is a Brahmin caste name; it was a pseudonym given by a Brahmin teacher of his. When joined with Bhimrao, however, it became his identity, completely changing its meaning in the process. Today Bhimrao has no meaning without Ambedkar.

Once, around 1980, my wife, Chanda, and I were returning to Chandrapur via Delhi, after a trip to Rajasthan. We had seats on the Pink City Express from Jaipur. Near us sat a prosperous-looking family, husband, wife, and two small children. We started talking and I learned that he was an officer in some ministry. We were chatting about the usual things. It was an atmosphere full of ease and gaiety. We fell to talking about the beauty of Rajasthan. My wife and the officer's wife were talking animatedly. Women are much faster in breaking down the wall of unfamiliarity. Suddenly, the subject of conversation changed midstream. The officer's wife asked my wife, "Bahenji, are you people Bengali?"

My wife replied easily, "No, we are from Uttar Pradesh. My husband is posted at the ordnance factory in Chandrapur."

"What is your caste?" The officer's wife fired her second question.

My wife's face changed color as soon as she heard the question. She looked at me. The atmosphere had been completely spoiled, as though a fly had fallen into a tasty dish. Before my wife could say anything, I replied, "Bhangi."[7]

As soon as they heard the word *Bhangi*, they lapsed into total silence. The two families did not communicate during the rest of the journey. A wall had come up between us, as though we had disturbed their enjoyment by encroaching on them through a trap door. The atmosphere had turned oppressive; the journey became very painful.

This is just one of many such incidents. Right from my childhood to this day, countless stings have stung not just my body but also my heart. What historical reasons lie behind this hatred and malice? Whenever I asked those who find the *varna* system ideal and take pride in Hindutva, instead of replying directly, they either avoid my question or get angry. They talk about *gyana*, or knowledge, in a convoluted vocabulary, but they will not accept the truth, that depriving human beings of human rights on account of their birth is not justifiable on any grounds. *Savarnas* harbor all sorts of preconceptions that make it impossible to develop normal personal relations with them.

Caste is a very important element of Indian society. As soon as a person is born, caste determines his or her destiny. Being born is not in the control of a person. If it were in one's control, then why would I have been born in a Bhangi household? Those who call themselves the standard-bearers of this country's great cultural heritage, did they decide which homes they would be born into? Of course, they turn to scriptures to justify their position, the

---

7. Bhangis are better known than Chuhras, who have the same caste status and occupation as Bhangis. Valmiki used the word *Bhangi* so that his listeners would have no doubt that he and his wife were untouchables.

scriptures that establish feudal values instead of promoting equality and freedom.

The *savarnas* constructed all sorts of mythologies: of chivalry, of ideals. What was the outcome? A defeated social order in the clutches of hopelessness, poverty, illiteracy, narrow-mindedness, religious inertia, and priestocracy, a social order embroiled in ritualism, which, fragmented, was repeatedly defeated by the Greeks, Shakas, Huns, Afghans, Moghuls, French, and English. Yet in the name of their valor and their greatness, *savarnas* kept hitting the weak and the helpless. Kept burning homes. Kept insulting women and raping them. To drown in self-praise and turn away from the truth, to not learn from history—what sort of a nation-building are they dreaming of?

Times have changed. But something somewhere continues to irk. I have asked many scholars to tell me why *savarnas* hate Dalits and Sudras, the lower castes, so much. The Hindus who worship trees and plants, beasts and birds, why are they so intolerant of Dalits? Today caste remains a preeminent factor in social life. As long as people don't know that you are a Dalit, things are fine. The moment they find out your caste, everything changes. The whispers slash your veins like knives. Poverty, illiteracy, broken lives, the pain of standing outside the door, how would the civilized *savarna* Hindus know it?

Why is my caste my only identity? Many friends hint at the loudness and arrogance of my writings. They insinuate that I have imprisoned myself in a narrow circle. They say that literary expression should be focused on the universal—a writer ought not limit himself to a narrow, confined terrain of life. That is, my being Dalit and arriving at a point of view according to my environment and my socioeconomic situation is being arrogant. Because in their eyes, I am only an SC, the one who stands outside the door.

GLOSSARY

abey (pronounced ahbey)—hey.

Abey, Chuhre (pronounced Ahbey, Churey)—Hey, you, Chuhre.

adi—literally, from the beginning.

adivasi—an indigenous person; aborigine.

ashtami—eighth day of a Hindu festival.

asprishya—untouchable.

avarnas—those outside the *varna* system; untouchables.

bahu—daughter-in-law.

baithak—the outer room or space that men use as an area to meet and chat.

barat—the bridegroom's party.

baratis—members of the bridegroom's party.

basti—literally, a settlement; place where people have settled in villages and in towns or squatted without official sanction in towns. Often people of the same caste live side by side.

behen—sister (whether by blood or courtesy).

bhabhi—older brother's wife.

bhaiyya—brother (whether by blood or courtesy).

Bhangi—untouchable.

biri—Indian cigarette, raw tobacco wrapped tightly around a piece of *sal* leaf.

Brahmanas—commentaries on the Vedas, the most sacred Hindu texts.

bua—father's sister, or paternal aunt.

chacha—father's younger brother.

chachi—wife of father's brother.

chandala—untouchable.

charpai—rope-string cot.

chaturdashi—the fourth day of a Hindu festival.

chaturvarna—four gradations in which castes are placed: Brahmins, Kshatriyas, Vaisyas, and Sudras, arranged in a hierarchical order.

chowdhurain—the landowner's wife.

chowdhuri—landowner.

dacoit—gang members who rob and murder.

Depressed Classes—British government term for those castes who were just above the Dalits, not untouchable but still very deprived; now referred as Other Backward Classes, or OBCs.

devi—goddess.

devta—god.

dwija—twice-born status of the upper castes after performing thread ceremony, or *upanayan.*

gauna—the ceremony marking consummation of the marriage, when the young bride is sent to the bridegroom's home; at the time of the wedding the bride may be too young for sexual relations.

ghazal—an Urdu lyrical poem, usually sung.

Gita—The Gita, or Bhagavad Gita, translates to English as the Song of God and originally was part of the epic called the *Mahabharata,* but it became a separate book many centuries ago and is perhaps the most sacred book of the Hindus, expounding the moral law.

goonda—hoodlum.

gotra—the name of a large kinship group of many families within a caste who supposedly share a common ancestor; the name must be given when any ritual is performed.

gur—molasses.

gurudakshina—teacher's tribute.

gyana—knowledge.

jamadar—sweeper.

Jatakas—roughly six hundred texts of Buddhist literature that focus on the incarnations of the Buddha before he attained Buddhahood and provide a wealth of social history.

jati—caste.

ji—suffix added to names as courtesy, as in *chachaji*.

jowar—coarse grain, like millet.

khaddar—handloom shirt.

kothi—a substantial house.

Maharshi—"great sage," someone who impresses by his wisdom and ethical standards.

maidan—huge open field; public park.

mama—mother's brother.

mausa—husband of father's sister.

murga—rooster position, formed by squatting on the haunches, then drawing the arms through the inner thighs and pulling the head down so the hands can grasp the ears; a painful, constricted position.

nanad—husband's sister.

nanad-bhabhi relationship—as used here, the affectionate relations between the wife and her sister-in-law (husband's sister), a relationship that traditionally is a source of great tension, as one is a daughter of the house and the other a daughter-in-law.

nat samrat—the best actor; literally, the emperor of the theater.

navami—ninth day of a Hindu festival.

OBCs—acronym Other Backward Classes, an official government designation for certain castes; see *Depressed Classes*.

parantha—a kind of fried bread sometimes stuffed with vegetables.

pattal—leaf plate.

phupi—husband of father's sister.

pooris—bread that is deep fried and puffs up when hot.

pradhan—village chief.

puchha—exorcism.

puja—worship of a deity or god in the form of a statue, an idol.

Ramayana—Sanskrit epic written by the poet Valmiki in the third century B.C.,

Ramcharitmanas—later version of the *Ramayana* that was written by Tuslidas and is popular in northern and central India.

sahib—a person who is in authority or of a higher social status.

samskara—Hindu rites and rituals that are a part of the upper-caste Hindu's life.

savarnas—those within the *varna* system.

Scheduled Caste (SC)—official term for untouchables entitled to benefits under affirmative action policies.

Scheduled Tribes (STs)—*adivasis*, or tribal people entitled to special benefits under affirmative-action policies.

shairi—Urdu poetry.

shakti puja—offering made to the mother goddess Durga.

shohare—father-in-law, used as abuse.

shuddhi—Hindu purification ceremony to reconvert Christian or Muslim converts.

tai—wife of father's older brother.

tandav—Lord Shiva's dance of destruction.

tantric—someone who knows traditional black magic and casts spells, practicing a debased form of the ancient art of tantra.

tau—father's older brother.

upanayana—the sacred thread ceremony.

varna—literally, color; gradation within the *chaturvarna* system.

vida—departure; here, bride's' departure to her husband's home.

yagna—fire ritual of animal sacrifices and gifts to Brahmins.